The **CaReeR Cowa**R**d's** Guide™ to

Career Advancement

**Sensible Strategies for
Overcoming Career
Fears**

jist
Works
America's Career Publisher®

Katy Piotrowski, M.Ed.

The Career Coward's Guide to Career Advancement

© 2009 by Katy Piotrowski

7321 Shadeland Station, Suite 200
Indianapolis, IN 46256-3923
Phone: 800-648-JIST   Fax: 877-454-7839   E-mail: info@jist.com

Visit our Web site at **www.jist.com** for information on JIST, free job search tips, tables of contents and sample pages, and ordering instructions for our many products!

See the back of this book for additional JIST titles and ordering information. Quantity discounts are available for JIST books. Have future editions of JIST books automatically delivered to you on publication through our convenient standing order program. Please call our Sales Department at 800-648-5478 for a free catalog and more information.

Trade Product Manager: Lori Cates Hand
Cover Designers: Trudy Coler and Alan Evans
Illustrator: Chris Sabatino
Interior Designer: Amy Adams
Page Layout: Toi Davis
Proofreaders: Laura Bowman and Paula Lowell
Indexer: Kelly Henthorne

Printed in the United States of America
14 13 12 11 10 09   9 8 7 6 5 4 3 2 1

Library of Congress Cataloging-in-Publication Data

Piotrowski, Katy, 1962-

   The career coward's guide to career advancement : sensible strategies for overcoming career fears / by Katy Piotrowski.

      p. cm.

   Includes index.

   ISBN 978-1-59357-393-5 (alk. paper)

1. Career development. 2. Vocational guidance. I. Title.

   HF5381.P547

   2009650.14--dc22

                          2008049585

ISBN 978-1-59357-393-5

About This Book

One of my favorite sayings is, "If you're not green and growing, you're ripe and rotten!" And in the realm of career development, this is especially true. Most of us feel at our best—making meaningful contributions, expanding ourselves professionally and personally—when we're advancing in our work.

The Career Coward's Guide to Career Advancement is all about how to create and achieve a professional-progress formula that's just right for you. From articulating what's most important, to defining a vision for your career future, you'll quickly and effectively determine the exact action steps you'll need to take to attain your career hopes and dreams. You'll also learn exactly *how* to implement and succeed with the plan you define.

Maybe you're interested in climbing the corporate ladder, moving up a rung or two in pay and responsibility. Or perhaps you're

more interested in modifying your existing career situation, to attain better work-life balance. Or it could be that you're interested in becoming a true master in your field, recognized by others as a highly credible expert. Or it might be that you're interested in launching your own enterprise and creating an entity that embodies everything you stand for professionally.

Whatever your career goal, *The Career Coward's Guide to*

Career Advancement was designed to help you accomplish your career goals as effectively as possible. All of the strategies in this guide have been tried and proven successful by career-advancement-minded professionals just like you.

Do you worry that you'll fail with your career advancement efforts? You're not alone. Fear is the single biggest factor holding back most of us from starting and reaching our career goals, yet this book was written just for the "Career Coward" in all of us—that small, scared part of us that is nervous about moving forward, but is willing to risk some tiny steps anyway.

Thank you for considering and choosing this book. I'm excited about the career progress you'll be able to achieve using the strategies described in its pages. Get ready for an exciting, rewarding experience.

As always, I wish you the best in all of your career adventures!

Your fan and supporter,

Katy P.

Dedication

*To my Grandpa Bobbett and Grandma Patrick,
who showed me through their own careers
that rewarding, balanced work can be achieved
through vision, focus, and persistence.*

Contents

Acknowledgments

Many thanks to the multitude of motivational and professional development speakers who accompanied me on my commute to work day after day, sharing their wisdom through my audio player. They gave me inspiration and ideas for continuing to advance professionally, and I have used their principles in my own life as well as shared them with my clients.

Thanks, also, to my dear, supportive clients—especially for the hopes and challenges they share with me. It is a joy to work with them and to learn from them every day.

As always, I have huge gratitude for my supportive team at JIST who help to make the book-publishing process easy and successful. Thanks especially to my editor, Lori Cates Hand, and my publicist, Selena Dehne.

Move Ahead in Your Career to Achieve Greater Results and Satisfaction

What does career advancement mean to you? After years of experiencing my own career highlights and frustrations, as well as observing and supporting the progress of thousands of career-counseling clients, I've come to define career advancement as getting closer and closer to your career ideal.

That is my goal for you with this book: helping you to get closer and closer to your career ideal, step by step, year after year. I've included my favorite strategies for career advancement in this book to equip you with the tools and techniques you'll need to succeed. The results will be rewarding and exciting, so let's get started.

How to Use This Book to Achieve Your Career Advancement Goals

The Career Coward's Guide to Career Advancement walks you through proven, step-by-step processes for overcoming your fears and making steady progress in your career. Each chapter in the book provides you with techniques that have been tried, tested, and perfected on thousands of other Career Cowards just like you. And to make this valuable information even more fun and easy to use, each chapter includes an at-a-glance "Risk It or Run From It" status box, providing you the following vital information:

- **Risk Rating:** From "No risk at all" to "This is a deal breaker!" you'll quickly see how harmless or hazardous each step will be.

- **Payoff Potential:** Find out what's in it for you if you do decide to take the risk and complete the step. The payoff may be enough to push you through any fear that's holding you back.

- **Time to Complete:** Whether it's a few minutes, a few hours, or longer, you'll know in advance how much time each activity will take.

- **Bailout Strategy:** Absolutely refuse to put in the time or take the risk for a particular step? You have other options; find out what they are.

- **The "20 Percent Extra" Edge:** Learn how braving the recommended steps will give you a significant advantage over your competition.

- **"Go For It!" Bonus Activity:** Feeling really courageous? Push your success even further with this suggested activity.

Each information-packed chapter also includes

- A how-to section, which provides clear, motivating instructions for each activity.

- Information about Why It's Worth Doing, which helps you understand the purpose behind each interviewing recommendation.

- Panic Point! highlights, which point out and troubleshoot areas Career Cowards find especially challenging.

- An encouraging Career Champ Profile, which describes a real-life example of a Career Coward who succeeded after conquering a career advancement challenge.

- The Core Courage Concept, which boils down the chapter's key points into an inspiring message.

- And a Confidence Checklist, which provides an at-a-glance review of the chapter's primary action items.

As you move through the chapters, you'll learn how to implement and succeed with the following proven career advancement process:

- **Consider a variety of career advancement options and formats.** From climbing the corporate ladder to climbing out of your cubicle to a more flexible at-home work arrangement, there are a variety of career advancement formats for you to contemplate and choose from.

- **Analyze your past career successes and frustrations, and create a motivating career advancement plan (CAP).** You'll review and examine past career highlights and frustrations, as well as articulate your top career and life priorities, allowing you to develop a motivating, rewarding future career advancement plan that is just right for you.

- **Learn about a variety of resources to support your career progress.** From Yellow Pages listings to the professor who taught one of your skill-building courses, this book describes countless tools and resources to help you boost your career advancement progress.

- **Implement your plan and act on golden opportunities.** As you put your CAP into action, exciting possibilities will begin to unfold. You may discover the chance to join an inspiring team, adjust your work arrangement to better fit your lifestyle, or move into a career area that's intriguing to you. Rather than let these opportunities slip by, you'll find out how to respond to them effectively.

- **Progress throughout your career lifetime.** Imagine experiencing one career accomplishment after another, building on each preceding success to achieve the next, and attaining higher and higher levels of career satisfaction. It's possible, through ongoing application of the principles in this book. You'll find out how to master the basics essential to career advancement success, as well as how to apply and adjust them throughout the life of your career.

It's going to be a fun, rewarding ride, so let's get started! Here's an example of one truly accomplished career champ who applied the principles in this book with outstanding success.

Career Champ Profile: Ava

From the start, Ava was determined to create a career that would be motivating and rewarding for her. She set herself up for success by completing a graduate degree in astronomy, with the idea of maybe one day teaching at a university. Yet in the process of completing her Ph.D., she decided that the politics and funding challenges of positions within academia didn't fit her life values. So after graduating, instead of pursuing a teaching position, she sought a position as a scientific project manager with a private corporation, in hopes that she would be rewarded for her ability to perform well, rather than for her ability to play the political games necessary to succeed in higher education.

For several years, Ava's career advancement plan worked beautifully for her. She landed positions of greater and greater responsibility within businesses, managing the development and launch of several challenging scientific projects and programs. Yet after a while, she realized that even though she'd tried to take herself out of the mainstream of organizational politics, it was a large part of the business world as well. Looking forward, Ava was motivated to find a way to keep advancing in her career, while sidestepping as much of the political hassles as possible.

Toward this goal, Ava networked with several leaders in her industry, learning about their professional paths and discovering several career possibilities potentially available to her. It was during one of these conversations that Ava learned about the option of working as an independent consultant, signing on with organizations and businesses to manage a specific project for a finite period of time. This format seemed highly appealing to Ava, as it would allow her to apply her strengths in project management, but also enable her to extricate herself from long-term political challenges once an assignment was completed.

In the next few years, Ava further aligned herself with some of the key decision makers in her industry. She eventually landed her first independent contractor assignment, earning double what she was paid as an employee and allowing her to set her own schedule while working from her beautiful home office.

Year after year, Ava has secured higher-paying, more attractive contracts to manage, taking her closer and closer to her career ideal. Now in her early 40s, Ava is paid handsomely for the 30 hours of expertise she invests each week in her projects, and is able to take long walks along a beautiful river near her home throughout the day. Although politics are still a part of her position, they are a minor aspect that Ava can step away from once an assignment is complete.

Ava isn't sure what the next chapter in her career advancement will bring, but she's keeping her attention on her long-term goals, steering her successes steadily toward her ideal.

Part 1

Create a Motivating, Customized Career Advancement Plan

Chapter 1

Consider Your Career Advancement Options

What does career advancement look like to you? Over the years, I've seen firsthand that career advancement is a concept that varies from person to person. As an example, at my office one day I had two back-to-back career counseling appointments. The first client had described her career advancement objective as, "I want to step back from my current level of responsibilities. Rather than being in charge of so many things, I want to specialize and reduce my stress." Her career advancement goal was to create more balance in her life. The other client stated his career progress goal as, "I want to move up in my company, to take on more responsibility." So when it comes to moving forward in a career, one person's distress may be another person's dream! In this chapter, I'll provide an overview of a variety of career progress options as a first step toward deciding which plan will be just right for you.

Risk It or Run From It?

- **Risk Rating:** No risk at all...you're just reading and considering.

(continued)

(continued)

- **Payoff Potential:** Excellent! This information will broaden your ideas about career advancement options that exist for you. Having more possibilities will ultimately help you make choices that are right for you.

- **Time to Complete:** As long as it takes you to read this chapter.

- **Bailout Strategy:** Well, you could skip over to chapter 2 without any huge negative consequences and begin completing those activities, but you run the risk of missing out on an idea or format for your career advancement plan that you might not have known about before, and that might be just right for you.

- **The "20 Percent Extra" Edge:** The vast majority of people coast down the path of life, responding to options as they pop up along the way. Very few take the time to answer, "What do I really want to create for myself?" The thought you put into your career advancement planning will allow you to achieve more of what you want, with less effort.

- **"Go For It!" Bonus Activity:** Spend some time thinking about career-minded professionals you admire. What advancement plan have they been following? If you're not sure, conduct a few informal interviews to learn more about their career advancement processes, providing you additional information for your own advancement.

How to Consider the Career Progress Possibilities That Are Available to You

There are so many ways to "advance" in your career: move into the next position on your career path, fine-tune your current job, start a sideline business, or do something completely different. The possibilities are endless! Following are several ideas for you to consider as options in your career advancement planning. After looking at the list of options, if you find yourself unsure of which format is most appropriate for you, complete the exercises in chapter 2 and then review this list again. You'll be equipped with more insight into your career goals and needs, and an effective career-advancement format will then become clearer to you.

Climb the Corporate Ladder

This is a popular dream for many…work hard, be noticed, and get bumped up to the next level in your organization. There are many advantages to this career advancement plan.

- If you love your current work, aiming for the next step on the path will allow you to learn more and grow within your specialty.

- Chances are, you already have a pretty clear picture of what this would look like, so you won't need to spend much time scoping out your career-progress vision.

- Moving up within your current line of work can lead to higher pay and status—pretty nice perks!

For you, moving up your current employer's corporate ladder might be just the career advancement result you're seeking.

Tweak Your Existing Work

Maybe you're not interested in climbing the legendary corporate ladder. Instead, you'd rather modify your current position to make it even better for you. For instance, maybe you want to work part time, rather than 40+ hours each week. Or spend more time on a certain aspect of your job responsibilities, and cut back on other tasks. Or simply move from your dingy cubicle to a space with a window. Whatever changes you want to make, you're not interested in scrapping your entire job…just overhauling it. By tweaking a factor here or there, you can make your on-the-job satisfaction skyrocket.

Expand into New Career Territories

Feeling a little flat about your work—but still like the majority of what it has to offer? What if you could find ways to boost your career contentment by adding in some new elements that would reenergize you and kick-start your professional growth? There are literally hundreds of ways to transform your ho-hum career into something more motivating and exciting. For instance, you could take a skill-building class that would open doors to new opportunities within your specialty. Or get involved with a professional association to help plan an upcoming conference, and in the process, meet several inspiring industry gurus. Or find innovative ways to execute your work, such as working from home, where you could connect more over the Internet, write articles, or lead webinars. Once you begin investigating ways to stretch your skills into new areas, you'll soon be faced with the (very fun!) challenge of deciding what to jump into first.

Swap One Career for Two or More

Do you slog through your job day after day, performing well and getting good feedback, but secretly longing for a little more variety? What if rather than having just one "loaf" of a career, you had two or more "muffins" that make up your daily work rations? Some of the happiest workers move from one type of work to another, all in the same day, week, or month. For example, you might work two days each week as a technical writer, two days as a gardener for hire, and one day as a teacher's helper at your local elementary school. There are several advantages to this "muffin" approach: If you lose one of your positions, you have other income streams to help carry you through. Or if one muffin starts to seem bland, you can dump it and try something new for a while. Rather than limiting yourself to a single career field, you can choose from a buffet of possibilities!

Take a Break for a Period of Time

In academia, it's typical for professors and head administrators to take a sabbatical—a break of up to six months—for rest, research, and rejuvenation. Sometimes they use this time away to spend dedicated time learning about a topic of interest to them that could ultimately benefit their work. This type of break may be just what you need to add new life to your career.

Tiptoe into an Entrepreneurial Venture

Or perhaps you're thinking, "I'm sick of working for 'The Man.' I have the expertise and talent needed to strike out on my own. I'm not ready to make a huge leap, but I'd like to start heading in the direction of owing my own business." Excellent idea! And, lucky for you, there are loads of ways to experiment with having your own enterprise before you take a huge leap. Thousands of sideline Internet businesses, as well as part-time product and service companies, are opening their doors each day. For just a minor investment of time, effort, and risk, you can test the waters for owning your own enterprise...and it may turn out to be the career progress formula you've been seeking!

Why It's Worth Doing

Not too long ago, I made a fun discovery at the meat counter at my local grocery store. I'd stopped by to pick up a flank steak to marinate and grill for guests who were coming the next day, but I was shocked at the per-pound price of the brand I wanted to buy. I stood there staring at the little orange sign at the front of the case, trying to decide what to do.

One of the butchers wandered over to where I was standing. "Can I help you?" he asked. I told him I'd had my heart set on flank steak, but that the price was making me choke. "Have you ever tried flap steak?" he asked. I shook my head no. "I personally like it better — it's more tender and flavorful, plus it's cheaper," he told me, pointing to a section in the case where the flap steaks were displayed. It looked a little different than any other meat I'd bought before, but not disturbingly different. "Okaaay..." I replied, "I'll give it a try." Turned out he was right — it was more delicious than flank steak, and less expensive! If I hadn't been open to other ideas, I never would have made this tasty (and budget friendly) culinary discovery.

Similarly, considering a range of career advancement possibilities *before* you decide on any one activity increases your chances for finding an option that truly meets your hopes and goals. Keep an open mind, and an option better than any you've dreamed of before may present itself.

Career Champ Profile: Reece

Reece took a deep breath and then launched into an explanation of his current career situation. "I run a great little construction business," he told me and the other members of our career development group, "but it just feels as if I'm missing something. Don't get me wrong…I love the company, what we do, who I work with…that's all good stuff. But I have skills and interests that I just don't feel that I'm paying enough attention to right now."

He continued: "I'd hate to give up this company, but I haven't figured out how I can get into something new without letting go of this business. I want to have my cake and eat it, too!" Talking further, we found out that Reece actually had quite a bit of flexibility in his schedule. "I have great managers to keep things running day to day, so I can take off for a few weeks at a time if I need to." After hearing about different formats for career advancement, Reece especially liked the idea of spending short stretches of time throughout the year on different career advancement projects, without needing to abandon his current business.

Over the next few months, Reece brainstormed and investigated options for tapping into those career possibilities. He looked into helping the local university transfer technologies it had developed to real-world use. He researched what it would be like to help inventors bring their products to market. He checked into taking baby boomers on experiential tours to international locations.

Ultimately, Reece connected with a management-training company who contracted with him to provide management-training seminars to companies in his region. This part-time career opportunity would allow Reece to make better use of his leadership skills—a talent he'd been underutilizing—plus he could work it into his current career, allowing him to, in his words, "have his cake and eat it, too!"

Core Courage Concept

Staying in your current career box might feel safe, but it's not necessarily comfortable. Chances are, you're pushing up against the confines of your current career arrangement, and feeling ready to stretch yourself farther. But what will this look like for you? With so many possibilities, it can feel overwhelming trying to decide on a career progress plan. Yet be kind to yourself; take this process one step at a time. For now, just consider which career advancement format seems to be the best fit for you. Take in the information and ponder the possibilities. The answers that are right for you will become clear to you in time.

Confidence Checklist

☐ Climb the corporate ladder.

☐ Tweak your existing work.

☐ Expand into new career territories.

☐ Swap one career for two or more.

☐ Take a break for a while.

☐ Tiptoe into an entrepreneurial venture.

Chapter 2

Define Your Career Advancement Priorities

With so many career advancement options available, making decisions about where to focus your time and energy can feel overwhelming. For this reason, it's helpful to begin with the basics—the skills and talents you love to use, the values by which you want to live your life—as a foundation for career advancement planning and decision making. In the next few pages, you'll have the opportunity to identify the skills and values most important to you to help in your career advancement planning.

Risk It or Run From It?

- **Risk Rating:** Pretty low. You'll just be analyzing the past to identify areas to focus on in the future.

- **Payoff Potential:** Excellent! This will help you create a strong foundation for your career advancement planning and execution.

- **Time to Complete:** About 30 minutes.

- **Bailout Strategy:** You can skip this chapter, and dive into putting together your first-draft career advancement plan in chapter 3. Buuuuuuuuut…geez, you might miss out on

(continued)

(continued)

identifying an important area for advancement that isn't immediately obvious to you. Your choice.

- **The "20 Percent Extra" Edge:** The world's greatest leaders will tell you that analyzing the past is one of the best ways to plan for the future. Take the time to study your own path to this point in your life, and you'll increase your chances for future successes.

- **"Go For It!" Bonus Activity:** Ask people who know you well—family members and close friends—to outline your career history, as they've observed it, to gather even more information about your experiences.

How to Assess Your Career Advancement Opportunities and Needs

Philosopher George Santayana once said, "Those who cannot remember the past are doomed to repeat it." In our life and career, it's easy to get stuck in the rut of repeating the same mistakes again and again. In this chapter, you'll have the chance to take an aerial snapshot of your career to this point to help you identify opportunities for improvement in the future—as well as identify pitfalls to avoid repeating. The following fun, easy steps will quickly show where to focus in the development of your initial career-advancement plan.

Analyze Your Past Career Successes and Frustrations

What has your career path looked like up until now? Chances are you've experienced highs and lows in your career...and you would rather set yourself up to achieve a greater number of "highs" in the future! To better understand how you've arrived at where you are today, as well as to maximize your chances for positive future successes, complete the following exercise to analyze your career history up until now:

- Jot down a timeline of major activities that have occurred in your work and career, listing the main highlights. Don't fret about making it fit any particular format, just list details that help you recall key aspects of your career experiences. As an example, here's mine:

  1. In high school, I worked on campaigns for fellow students who were running for class offices. I decided then that I wanted to be an advertising specialist.

  2. I completed a degree in Advertising Communications from University of Tennessee.

  3. I landed a job with First Software as an advertising copywriter.

  4. From there, I moved on to other marketing positions with Raster Technologies, Numerix, Alliant, and Mercury Computer Systems. About eight years into my marketing career, work started to feel hollow and meaningless. I decided to investigate other careers and decided to move into career counseling.

  5. I completed a master's degree in career counseling from Colorado State University.

  6. I landed a position with Haldane & Associates as a career advisor.

  7. Three years later, I opened my own career counseling practice.

  8. Eight years later, I got a little burned out on the intensity of one-on-one career counseling, and investigated doing my work differently.

  9. I launched group counseling services and sought out opportunities to write more, including submitting a proposal and landing a contract to write five *Career Coward's* books.

10. I sought out a co-owner for my career counseling practice to help me grow it further.

Panic Point! Yikes! Are you just getting started on your career path, and are you worrying that you don't have many career steps to include on your list? If this sounds like you, keep in mind that it doesn't really matter how *many* points you have listed on your timeline. We're just taking a snapshot of your situation up to now to help you decide where to go from here. Write down what you can think of right now, understanding that you can add in more later.

- Now, using a 1–10 scale, rate the events on your timeline based on how energized or frustrated you felt at that time, with "1" marking times when you felt especially low and discouraged and "10" marking times of high energy and satisfaction. Here are my ratings:

  - In high school, I worked on campaigns for fellow students who were running for class offices. I decided then that I wanted to be an advertising specialist. *8*

  - I completed my degree in Advertising Communications from University of Tennessee. *7*

  - Landed a job with First Software as an advertising copywriter. *8*

  - Moved on to other marketing positions with Raster Technologies, Numerix, Alliant, and Mercury Computer Systems. About eight years into it, work started to feel hollow and meaningless. *1*

  - I decided that I wanted to move into career counseling, and I completed a master's degree from Colorado State University. *9*

- I landed a position with Haldane & Associates as a career advisor. *6*

- Three years later, I opened my own career counseling practice. *7*

- Eight years later, I got a little burned out on the intensity of one-on-one career counseling, and investigated doing my work differently. *2*

- I launched group counseling services and sought out opportunities to write more, including submitting a proposal and landing a contract to write five *Career Coward's* books. *9*

- I sought out a co-owner for my career counseling practice to help me grow it further. *8*

- Next, analyze why you were feeling the way you were feeling during the peaks and lows. For instance, looking at my ratings, I remember feeling especially motivated when I worked on my master's degree and when I wrote my book proposal for the *Career Coward's* series, because I was learning and applying new information and techniques on a topic I love: career counseling.

On the flip side, my low points happened when I was working in high tech as a marketing specialist, and when I was slogging through what felt like an endless line of seeing career counseling clients one-on-one. Looking back, those were times when I had very little new learning and creativity going on. Instead, my days were filled with tasks that felt repetitive or meaningless. What was going on during the peaks and valleys of your career timeline? Make notes about important insights.

Obtain an Objective Assessment of Your Top Skills and Talents

Sometimes we're blind to our best skills and talents. While others may clearly see the strengths we bring to our work and careers, we may be in the dark about exactly what our best assets are. For this

reason, I recommend completing a standardized strengths or apti-
tudes assessment at some time in your career. These are a few of my
favorite resources for this purpose:

- *The Career Coward's Guide to Changing Careers:* This book, by
  yours truly, includes several activities for defining your
  top strengths and values. It also includes ways to apply those
  priorities in a number of successful and rewarding career
  situations.

- **StrengthsFinder:** Developed by Gallop Research, this online
  assessment takes about 20 minutes to complete and will
  produce a descriptive listing of your top five strengths. I've
  given this assessment to hundreds of my own clients, and in
  practically every case, they found the results to be accurate and
  confidence boosting. To access this assessment, you'll need to
  purchase the *StrengthsFinder 2.0* book and use the online assessment access code included. Then, once you've defined your
  strengths, you can identify a multitude of ways to capitalize on
  them using a book such as Marcus Buckingham's *Now Go Put
  Your Strengths to Work*.

- **Johnson O'Connor or Highlands aptitude/natural abilities
  testing:** These two test batteries provide a scientific measure-
  ment of the innate capabilities you were born with. For
  example, when I completed the Johnson O'Connor test batteries, I learned that a) I'm great at generating ideas, and b) I'd
  suck at being a brain surgeon, because my fine motor abilities
  are terrible. Knowing which skill areas you naturally excel in
  can help you decide how you want to maximize your potential.

Itemize What You Prioritize in Your Career

Now that you've listed and rated the major career events in your life,
as well as defined the top skills you want to maximize in your career
activities, take a few minutes to itemize your top professional priorities. Consider the highs and lows of your career, as well as what you
were focusing on—or neglecting—at various times in your life. Also

ask yourself, "What holes do I need to work on filling now?" Following is a list of several values to help you articulate your top priorities today. While there are most likely several values on this list that are important to you, aim to identify the top 5 to 10 that are *most* related to your career situation right now. It might make sense for you to do this activity in two steps:

1. Highlight *all* of the values that seem important to you.

2. Organize the highlighted values based on their priorities for you.

Abundance	Balance
Acceptance	Beauty
Accomplishment	Being the best
Accuracy	Belonging
Achievement	Bravery
Activeness	Calmness
Adaptability	Camaraderie
Adventure	Capability
Affection	Carefulness
Affluence	Celebrity
Altruism	Challenge
Ambition	Charm
Amusement	Cheerfulness
Appreciation	Clarity
Assertiveness	Cleanliness
Attentiveness	Cleverness
Attractiveness	Closeness
Availability	Comfort

Commitment	Dependability
Compassion	Determination
Completion	Devoutness
Composure	Dexterity
Concentration	Diligence
Confidence	Discipline
Connection	Discovery
Consciousness	Diversity
Consistency	Drive
Contentment	Duty
Contribution	Dynamism
Control	Eagerness
Conviction	Education
Coolness	Effectiveness
Cooperation	Efficiency
Correctness	Empathy
Courage	Encouragement
Courtesy	Endurance
Craftiness	Energy
Creativity	Enjoyment
Credibility	Entertainment
Cunning	Enthusiasm
Curiosity	Excellence
Daring	Excitement
Decisiveness	Exhilaration

Expediency	Heart
Expertise	Helpfulness
Exploration	Heroism
Expressiveness	Honesty
Fairness	Honor
Faith	Humility
Fame	Humor
Family	Independence
Fearlessness	Insightfulness
Fidelity	Inspiration
Financial independence	Integrity
Fitness	Intelligence
Flexibility	Intensity
Focus	Intimacy
Freedom	Introversion
Friendliness	Intuition
Frugality	Inventiveness
Fun	Investing
Generosity	Joy
Giving	Justice
Gratitude	Kindness
Growth	Knowledge
Happiness	Leadership
Harmony	Learning
Health	Liberation

Liveliness	Power
Logic	Practicality
Longevity	Pragmatism
Love	Precision
Loyalty	Privacy
Making a difference	Proactivity
Mastery	Professionalism
Mellowness	Prosperity
Meticulousness	Reason
Mindfulness	Reasonableness
Modesty	Recognition
Motivation	Relaxation
Obedience	Reliability
Open-mindedness	Religiousness
Optimism	Resilience
Organization	Resourcefulness
Originality	Respect
Passion	Richness
Peace	Sacrifice
Perfection	Security
Perkiness	Self-reliance
Persistence	Service
Persuasiveness	Sharing
Philanthropy	Shrewdness
Popularity	Sincerity

Skillfulness	Thoroughness
Solitude	Traditionalism
Spirit	Trust
Spirituality	Truth
Spontaneity	Understanding
Stability	Uniqueness
Strength	Unity
Structure	Usefulness
Success	Variety
Support	Vision
Sympathy	Wealth
Synergy	Wisdom
Teamwork	Zeal

Panic Point! Do you see *many* values on this list that are important to you? Does the idea of narrowing them down to only 5 or 10 seem too limiting? Although there will be many values that are significant to you, chances are that at this very second, there are some that are higher on your priority list—areas in your life that need more urgent attention. *Those* are the 5 to 10 values that you want to focus on today for career-planning purposes. In the future, when you've given these initial areas the attention they need, you'll be able to move them down the list a little and replace them with different values. So you don't really need to eliminate any values—just put them in an order based on your highest needs at the moment.

For instance, writing this today, I would list my top five values as these:

1. Family

2. Health

3. Creativity

4. Balance

5. Integrity

Define What Your Top Values Mean to You in Your Career

As a final step in this values exercise, write a few sentences about what each of your top 5 to 10 values means to you. To the best of your ability, write about what you hope to create for yourself in your career and life in each area. Defining your values might feel a little "idealistic," but do your best to jot down some of your key thoughts. What you define as your ideals related to your top values will play a large part in defining your career advancement plan. As an example, here are my definitions:

- **Family:** My goal is to develop and maintain an environment where my immediate family members—husband, children, and myself—feel safe and loved and where we are able to achieve our potentials. This includes a good deal of time spent together enjoying each other's company in an environment that is nurturing and energizing. I also aim to extend this support to our good friends and extended family, creating a large, loving network.

- **Health:** In this arena, the objective is to achieve and maintain physical, mental, and financial health through wise, day-to-day pursuits. This includes defining and executing motivating health goals, measuring results, and tweaking activities, resulting in abundant, life-sustaining results.

- **Creativity:** My aim is to devote adequate time and resources to creative activities, including writing, performing, knitting, cooking, and making crafts, to a point where I feel my creative talents are being used adequately and in areas that are meaningful and energizing to me. From a career standpoint, this means staying involved in activities such as writing books, creating and delivering presentations, and designing my office space and materials in pleasing and stimulating ways.

- **Balance:** At most times in my life (with a few exceptions due to crises) I put an appropriate amount of time and energy into the areas that are most important to me: family, health, creativity, and integrity. This is an ongoing effort, requiring careful attention to the balance at any given time and the making of necessary adjustments.

- **Integrity:** Someone once defined integrity as "Doing the right thing, even when no one else is watching." This is my goal for how I live my life.

Once you've defined what those values mean to you, give yourself a little pat on the back. You've just developed a very valuable foundation for successful career planning.

Why It's Worth Doing

Habit is one of the most powerful forces in our lives. To prove this point, pay attention to how much your routine drives what you do when you wake up tomorrow morning. What do you do first, second, and so on? How do you make the coffee? Brush your teeth? Get dressed? Chances are, you don't even really think about these activities as you begin your day. Your habits put those tasks on autopilot, and routine decisions happen pretty much without your awareness.

Habits can be powerful assets, or ball-and-chain liabilities that drag us back into the same frustrating routines over and over. For example, I had fallen into the same routine of checking my e-mail every morning as soon as I got to my office. My routine was to walk in, put away my purse, turn on my computer, and check my e-mail. If e-mail was the *most* important activity on my list, this habit would be a good one to sustain. Yet for me, e-mail is rarely the *most* important activity on the day's agenda. So rather than putting it first day after day, I made a conscious choice to change my habit, and to instead begin the day by rereading my plan for where I want to take my career, business, and life—a more productive habit to adopt.

Your habits in your career might drive you, unconsciously, in the wrong direction. By taking the time to analyze your top priorities, and what you want to create for yourself in your career, you increase your chances for achieving more successful career results in the future.

Career Champ Profile: Alva

Alva had worked as a project manager for ten years, managing the development of complex technical projects for various employers. She was good at her specialty, but after a decade of pouring her time and energy into her work, she was beginning to feel burned-out. "I want to make some changes for the better in my career, but I'm not sure what to focus on."

As a starting point, I asked Alva to create a timeline of her career milestones. She listed completing her mechanical engineering degree, then taking her first job working for a defense contractor, later moving into her first project manager position, and then taking three other project management jobs in a row since then. During her second project manager position, she had also completed an MBA.

I asked her to point out the high and low points in her timeline. "I hated working as a mechanical engineer right out of school…it was too detailed," she began. "But my first project management position was a real high point for me. I loved orchestrating all of the pieces involved in getting a project completed." She pointed out another low point—when she felt micromanaged by a boss—as well as another peak—when she took on a development project that was much larger than any she'd run before.

"Now look over this list of values and let me know which five to ten feel like the highest priority values for you right now." Alva took a few minutes to study the list, her highlighter poised over the paper. "*Independence* is definitely one of them," she began. She also highlighted *Intelligence*, *Growth*, *Mindfulness*, and *Balance*.

I asked her to define what *Mindfulness* meant to her. "I want to be involved in work that is responsible to our planet, not harming any living thing. It bothers me that most of the projects I work on now are defense related. I'd like to change that."

As homework, Alva defined what her other priority values meant to her. We talked a week later. "This is a first step toward creating your career advancement plan. How are you feeling?" Alva let out a sigh of relief. "Great! I've had these things floating around in my head for months, but I wasn't doing anything concrete with them. Now I feel as if at least I'll be paying better attention to what's important to me and making plans that will incorporate my priorities. I'm excited!"

Core Courage Concept

Taking a hard look at what's been working (as well as what hasn't!) takes guts. Discovering that you keep falling into the same routine of frustrating experiences again and again can feel like a punch in the stomach. But being aware of your less-than-helpful habits is the first step toward improving them. Be patient with yourself as you digest what you discovered about your career path to this point, and before you know it, a better plan will begin to come together.

Confidence Checklist

☐ Analyze your past career successes and frustrations.

☐ Obtain an objective assessment of your top skills and talents.

☐ Itemize what you value in your career.

☐ Define what your top values mean to you.

Chapter 3

Develop an Initial Career Advancement Plan

C hances are that, after having read and completed the exercises in chapter 2, you're starting to feel a little excited about creating your own career advancement plan. Clues about what you want to achieve, and activities you want to accomplish, are starting to come to you in bits and pieces. In this chapter, we'll take your plan development one step further, showing you how to put together a rough draft. It's easy and fun, so let's get started!

Risk It or Run From It?

- **Risk Rating:** Because this is just a rough draft of a plan, the risk is low. You can always refine (or completely change) your plan later.

- **Payoff Potential:** Priceless! Defining a few initial goals (even if you'll modify them later) will save you from wasting time and energy trying to figure out which way to go.

- **Time to Complete:** A half hour or so.

- **Bailout Strategy:** If you completed the activities in chapter 2, you could get away with skipping this step if you feel strapped for time.

(continued)

(continued)

> - **The "20 Percent Extra" Edge:** Putting in the time and energy to write out an actual plan for your career progress will allow you to think through your strategy more carefully so that, ultimately, your results will be better.
>
> - **"Go For It!" Bonus Activity:** Create a career advancement plan binder with sections—values, skills, strategy, action items, schedules, etc.—dedicated to the plan information most essential to your future career satisfaction.

How to Create a First-Draft Career Advancement Plan

Congrats! You've already completed some important steps toward putting together your initial career advancement plan (CAP): You've considered different progress formats, as described in chapter 1, and defined your top-priority values and goals in chapter 2. Now you'll put these pieces together to create a starter advancement strategy.

Speculate on Which Career Advancement Plan Format You Want to Choose

Since reading the list of several career advancement formats to consider in chapter 1, which potential strategy seems most on target for you? Is it moving higher up within your current career, or modifying or expanding your present position work so that it's a better fit for you? Or how about engaging in multiple jobs or positions, or launching your own business? Or perhaps it's another idea that isn't even listed here. Whatever format seems most on target for you, take time now to write down your initial career advancement goal, along with a few sentences about what you want potential plans to look like. The following are some examples.

Move Up Within Your Current Career

"In the next year or so, I want to be promoted to manager within my department. I want to take over responsibility for leading our team of specialists. This might mean moving to a different location, where an opportunity is available, and I'm okay with that. With this promotion, I want to negotiate a 25 percent increase in pay. Then, a few years from now, I'd like to be promoted to regional director."

Modify Your Existing Work to Make It a Better Fit for You

"Three to six months from today, I want to have worked out an arrangement with my employer where I can work from home three to four days each week. I want my employer to set me up with equipment at home so that I can do my work by telecommuting. As part of this plan, I want to offload the in-person, client-support meetings that I currently handle, and take on more tele-support responsibilities, to balance things out."

Expand into New Territory Within Your Existing Work

"Because I love the financial analysis part of my work, I want to find more ways to be involved with this activity. I want my manager to teach me more about what she does in this aspect of the business, and maybe take a class or two. Over time, I'd like to take on more of the financial responsibilities for the company."

Trade One Career for Two or More

"I am skilled in technical writing, and I want to maintain a career in this specialty, but only part time. This would mean that I'd need to work with my present employer to figure out how I can cut back to working 25 to 30 hours each week. Then, during the time that will be freed up, I want to find a part-time job creating stained glass windows. Ultimately, I would have two careers: technical writer and stained glass artist."

Take a Sabbatical

"I've been plugging away diligently at my career for years, and taking a step back for four to six months would allow me to rejuvenate myself; do some reading, research, and exploration; and gain a fresh perspective on where I want to go from here. When I return, I would be able to bring new energy and innovative viewpoints to the organization."

Launch Your Own Business

"I'm strongly motivated to start my own landscaping design business. The 15 years I've spent working for companies in this field have prepared me well for being on my own. So, in the next 24 months, I want to create a plan, save some start-up funds, and then go out on my own."

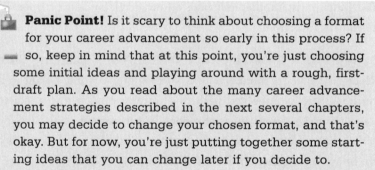

Panic Point! Is it scary to think about choosing a format for your career advancement so early in this process? If so, keep in mind that at this point, you're just choosing some initial ideas and playing around with a rough, first-draft plan. As you read about the many career advancement strategies described in the next several chapters, you may decide to change your chosen format, and that's okay. But for now, you're just putting together some starting ideas that you can change later if you decide to.

My rough-draft career advancement goal, for instance, would be this:

"I want to keep progressing in my current line of work. I want to grow my career counseling practice, helping more clients through activities that help them achieve their career goals more effectively and successfully. I also want to continually develop myself within the field of career counseling, always improving my credentials and knowledge."

Create a List of Career Needs and Opportunities

Now that you've settled on an initial idea for your CAP format, it's time to think through some possible components to include in your plan. You'll be happy to know that you've already done much of the hard work on this one. To begin, pull out your list of prioritized values and the definitions you created for each of them from chapter 2. As a reminder, the prioritized values list I created for myself included Family, Health, Creativity, Balance, and Integrity. Look at your own list and ask yourself, "What could I do to get closer to my ideal picture?" Create a long list of possible ideas, without worrying about how (or if) you'll actually act on any of them.

Let's use one of my value definitions as an example:

Health — In this arena, the objective is to achieve and maintain physical, mental, and financial health, through wise, day-to-day pursuits. This includes defining and executing motivating health goals, measuring results, and tweaking activities, resulting in abundant, life-sustaining outcomes.

On the day that I'm writing this, I see the following opportunities to get closer to my ideal picture:

"Achieve and maintain physical, mental, and financial health through wise, day-to-day pursuits...." This is a pretty big statement, so I'll break my overall value into smaller pieces and think through each aspect one at a time:

- **Physical health:** Right now, I am in pretty good shape physically. Besides, my career is not directly tied to my physical activities, although it's important for me to be healthy.

- **Mental health:** My mental well-being is alright, although I'll admit that I struggle with some of the mental challenges tied to growing a business and becoming a successful author. What would help with these challenges? Maybe...

  - Continue to participate in the monthly mentoring group of which I'm a member. The 11 other business owners in the group give me great ideas for growing a healthy business.

- Research a few professional associations that would be made up of business owners in a similar industry to mine: career services. Maybe join and become an active member.

- Maybe take a course, or read some books, on effective ways to publicize my books.

- Maybe research some authors whose books have done extremely well, and find out how they grew the success of their books.

- Maybe work with my publicists more actively to identify ways that I can improve the sales results of my books.

Thinking about actually acting on these ideas makes me feel more optimistic about my mental state regarding my career. These ideas might be good to somehow include in my plan.

- **Financial health:** Overall, I do okay financially, but it doesn't feel as if I have a good plan for how to keep my overall financial picture healthy. Maybe I could do the following:

    - Create some goals for what I want my financial picture to look like.

    - Take a few classes, or read a few books, to learn more about how to better manage my finances as well as other priorities related to money management that I need to know.

    - Schedule a few hours each month to review my financial status against my goals and determine any action items I need to take in the next month.

    - Increase the financial value of what I have to offer the world by investing in myself with further education — maybe a Ph.D.

Panic Point! Are you looking at what I've written for my list of potential activities and thinking "I know I have holes in my plan, but I'm clueless about how to even begin filling those holes. She's writing down all of these ideas—I don't know where to begin!" Okay, okay—fair enough. But notice that my financial health ideas are more vague than my mental health ideas, simply because I know a *little* more about what I should consider doing related to publicizing my books. Vague ideas at this stage of your career advancement planning process are just fine. So if all you can write is "Figure out what I need to do to get closer to my ideal," that'll do!

As you can see, by using just one of my values definitions and figuring out what I want to do to work toward achieving it, I've started to create a list of ideas to build into my CAP.

By repeating this same process with my other four goals, I would very quickly be able to create a nice starter list of plan components.

So now it's your turn; pick one of your values definitions from chapter 2, and ask yourself, "What could I do to get closer to my ideal picture?" Create a list of possible activities, even if they're just vague ideas at this point. In the next several chapters, we'll cover several strategies that will help you define those ideas more specifically and then achieve them.

Put Together a Starting Strategy

This step will be easy, sneezy, because you've already written most of it. Simply combine the two components you created in the previous two steps in this chapter:

1. Your initial CAP format objective

2. Your ideas for getting closer to your career value ideals

Label the first part "Objective" and the second part "Action Plan." Here's what mine now looks like, with even more of my career-related-values action components added in:

Objective:

I want to keep progressing in my current line of work. I want to grow my career counseling practice, helping more clients through activities that help them achieve their career goals more effectively and successfully. I also want to keep developing myself within the field of career counseling, improving my credentials and knowledge.

Action Plan:

- Continue to participate in the monthly mentoring group of which I'm a member. The 11 other business owners in the group give me great ideas for growing a healthy business.

- Research a few professional associations that would be made up of business owners in a similar industry to mine: career services. Maybe join and become an active member.

- Maybe take a course, or read some books, on effective ways to publicize my books.

- Maybe research some authors whose books have done extremely well, and find out how they grew the success of their books.

- Maybe work with my publicists more actively to identify ways that I can improve the sales results of my books.

- Create some goals for what I want my financial picture to look like.

- Schedule a few hours each month to review my financial status against my goals, and determine any action items I need to take in the next month.

- Continue writing and creating career materials such as books, articles, and tools.

- Complete my Licensed Professional Counselor credential.

- Investigate the logistics and worth of getting a Ph.D. in a related field.

- Maintain a successful balance of work and home activities, regularly reevaluating the needs of each by conferring with the key people in my life.

- Set up quality-checking systems to ensure that the work my business performs for clients maintains my desired levels of integrity.

Wow, this is looking pretty good already, and we're just getting started. Hopefully you're feeling as optimistic about your first-draft CAP. And in the next few chapters, we'll make this plan even more specific, and achievable, for you.

Why It's Worth Doing

Christopher Columbus believed the world was round, and he was motivated to check out his theory. He wasn't exactly sure of what he would discover or how he would handle challenges that would pop up during his adventure, but he put together an initial plan and got started anyway.

Similarly, you have an idea (even if it's just a rough one) of how you want to progress in your career. You might not be crystal clear on what you're aiming for, but you're motivated to forge ahead anyway. By putting together a rough-draft career advancement plan, you have at least defined what you hope to accomplish. The specific details—and a better plan—will be revealed along the way.

Career Champ Profile: Ryanne

Ryanne was great at managing people and programs, and at attaining organizational growth objectives. But after nearly 20 years of helping other business owners achieve their growth goals, she wanted to be accomplishing great things for her own business. "I want to launch my own business venture...sorta," she told me during a counseling session. "But I'm not interested in starting something from scratch. Rather, I'd like to find a nice little business that could be much bigger, and buy in as a part owner. Then I'd help that business—my *own* business—grow."

Ryanne decided on her top values—wisdom, prosperity, health, leadership, and helpfulness—and wrote definitions for them. Then she brainstormed several action items related to her ideals. This is how her initial plan turned out:

Objective:

Find a small business with good growth opportunities, buy into it, and be a key part of helping it grow.

Initial Action Plan:

- Research a number of businesses that could benefit from my expertise and wisdom, and whose line of work would be challenging to me.

- Analyze the financial picture of several businesses to determine which offer the best potential for long-term, growing profitability.

- Evaluate the ownership and culture of various businesses to identify a few where I would be able to maintain a healthy mental and physical lifestyle.

- Also evaluate the products and/or services of those businesses to ensure that they are a good match for how I want to help others.

- Make offers to buy into an attractive business, proposing my role as a leader of people and programs, to help the business grow in prosperity.

When she was done putting together her initial career action plan, Ryanne sighed with relief. "Wow, it feels so good to put some of these things on paper, even if I'm not exactly sure of where I'm going or how I'll get there. But this at least gives me a little bit of a map for where to begin."

Core Courage Concept

The act of putting on paper an initial plan for what you hope to accomplish as you move forward in your career takes guts — especially for Career Cowards. The worries of "But what if I can't actually accomplish this plan" and "What if there's a better plan that I'll miss out on if I start with this one" can creep into your thoughts, causing you to second-guess yourself. Yet keep in mind that, at this point, *everything* — your entire plan — can be changed. You're simply giving yourself a place to begin progressing from here…and that can feel awesome.

Confidence Checklist

- ☐ Speculate on which career format you want to choose.
- ☐ Create a list of career needs and opportunities.
- ☐ Put together a starting strategy.

Part 2

Choose and Use Tools to Achieve Your Plan

Chapter 4

Create Your List of Target Customers, Employers, and Contacts

You've just created a rough draft of your CAP (career advancement plan), and now it's time to put some meat behind your strategy. As a first (and extremely important) step, I'll walk you through how to develop a list of people and organizations you might want to connect with to achieve your career advancement goals.

Risk It or Run From It?

- **Risk Rating:** Small. This is an information-gathering activity that carries very little possibility for harm or distress to you.

- **Payoff Potential:** Outstanding! Take the time now to identify people and places who can support attainment of your career advancement goals, and you'll save yourself from going down dead-end paths later.

- **Time to Complete:** At least an hour. But once you get started, you may discover how helpful and energizing this activity is and decide to devote even more time.

(continued)

(continued)

- **Bailout Strategy:** If you're crystal-clear on how one person or organization can support your CAP, you can begin by tapping into that resource, and then come back to this chapter later to identify even more helpful contacts.

- **The "20 Percent Extra" Edge:** Most of us have a wealth of resources available in the wings waiting to be noticed. The inventory of resources you list in this chapter will give you an excellent start in tapping those resources and accomplishing your CAP.

- **"Go For It!" Bonus Activity:** As you identify the types of people resources you'll need to successfully implement your CAP, contact people you trust to ask for their opinions on individuals and organizations to add to your list of potential sources.

How to Identify People and Places to Help You Achieve Your Plan

You know what you want to achieve with your CAP, and connecting with helpful contacts and companies will help you achieve those goals faster and easier. The following activities will show you how to identify the sources of support that are ideal for you.

Determine Individuals and Businesses You Need to Know

Whether you're aiming for a raise or raising the bar on services to offer your customers, creating a list of the key companies and decision makers around you will significantly boost your progress. Scope out people and places to consider by looking through your CAP, action item by action item, and ask yourself the following:

- Who will be directly involved in making it possible for me to succeed?

- Which people or businesses are in some way connected to the goals I've set for myself?

Let's take Ryanne's CAP from chapter 3 as an example. As a reminder, her progress goal was to find a small business with good growth opportunities, buy into it, and be a key part of helping it grow. One of Ryanne's action items is to research several businesses whose work would be challenging to her. Who would be directly involved in making it possible for her to succeed? Here are a few ideas:

- Business owners who are looking for a partner

- A banker who would help her fund her deal

- Her husband who would need to support the business she wanted to buy into

Moving on to the next question, "Which types of people or businesses are in some way connected to the goals I've set for myself?" allows Ryanne to identify even more target people and places:

- Her local chamber of commerce

- Commercial bankers knowledgeable about local businesses

- A business broker who represents companies

- Bob S., a man from Ryanne's health club who is a member of the local chamber

- Karly T., the branch manager at her bank

- Simon B., a friend who recently talked with a business broker

- David C., Ryanne's investment advisor who works with several small business owners

- Dana K., a business consultant that Ryanne's friend Lisa works with

- Arden M., a business owner Ryanne talked with at a cocktail party last month, who was talking about wanting to grow his business

You can see how easy it is to create a nice starter list of potential contacts for your target list, just by answering a few questions.

Panic Point! Are you fretting, "This doesn't seem so easy to *me!* I'm clueless about the people and places who would be able to impact my career advancement goals." It can seem a little overwhelming to try and think of specific places and people, especially if your current network of contacts is pretty limited. If this is your situation, keep your list more general, as in, "Hiring managers who work at advertising agencies," or "People who know about other small businesses in my area." This type of list is fine as you get started, and you can refine it later on in the process. You might also want to be sure that you've defined your career advancement goals clearly enough. Fuzzy goals make it difficult to see your path—and your target contacts and organizations—clearly. Review the exercises in chapters 1 and 2 again or read *The Career Coward's Guide to Changing Careers* for several additional ideas on clarifying your career focus.

Often, the people and places you might want to consider will fall into one or more of these categories:

- **"Hub" contacts:** These are individuals whose work puts them in contact with many people from a variety of backgrounds. Insurance, investment, and real estate brokers, as well as community leaders and bankers, frequently make excellent hub contacts to support your CAP.

- **Related-service providers:** Organizations and people who fall into this category are likely to be connected to your goal in some way that provides them a profit. For example, if you're looking to climb the corporate ladder, it would make sense for you to connect with recruiters in your current industry. And in Ryanne's case, because she wants to find a business to buy into, bankers and business brokers would be service providers related to her goal.

- **Direct decision makers:** Bottom line, the person or people who can say "yea" or "nay" to your career advancement goals are your direct decision makers. Want to add another line of work to your career? Then the hiring managers at the places where you'd like to work will be your direct decision makers. Want to change your current work schedule from five 8-hour days to four 10-hour days? Your current boss (maybe even her boss) will be the decision maker you'll need to convince.

Evaluate Formal Data Sources

Off the top of your head, you may have been able to list a number of people and places connected to your career goals. Yet chances are you've identified only a small portion of the organizations and individuals who would be able to help you implement your CAP. By evaluating more formal resources, you can greatly expand your list—and your potential for achieving what you want. These data resources might be helpful to you:

- **Yellow Pages listings, either online or hardcopy:** www.yellowpages.com and www.dexknows.com are two Web sites that can help you identify companies related to your CAP.

- **Local business directories, accessed online or through your area library:** Many cities collect and publish their own directories of business information. These resources will often list decision makers' names as well.

- **Professional association membership directories:** Associations related to your specialty or industry might offer a directory of the names of its members.

- **Product or service catalogs:** Similar to professional association directories, catalogs that list suppliers of products and services in line with your career goals can provide quick access to target people and companies.

- **Business databases such as Hoovers or Dow Jones:** Check out www.hoovers.com or www.dowjonesfactiva.com to see how useful their information may be to you.

- **Your current employer's employee directory:** A wealth of information and contacts may be as close as your own company's employee directory, especially if your career advancement goal is to move up—or around—within your current company.

As an example, Ryanne could quickly expand the list of businesses she might consider buying into by reviewing those listed in the Yellow Pages categories that interest her. And if it's your goal to move up one rung on the corporate ladder, then a professional association membership directory, or a product and service catalog listing key competitors in your industry, would help you easily discover many other potential places to target for work.

Create a Resource Database

Now that you've started identifying people and places who might be able to help you achieve your career advancement goals, be sure to record key information about them. Choose whatever info-collection tool you like best, from a handwritten notebook of information to a streamlined electronic database customized to your needs or anything else in between. A word processing file, spreadsheet, or Outlook file might work well for you. For the companies and contacts on your list, aim to gather and record the following information:

- Organization/Contact name

- Address

- Phone, e-mail

- Summary of its purpose, mission, products, and services

- Key decision makers, particularly those related to your career advancement goals (such as the Director of Sales, if you're seeking a position as a sales representative)

- Bonus information, such as recent announcements provided on the company's Web page or through news sources such as the newspapers

Why It's Worth Doing

A voice in your head might be thinking, "Is it really necessary to do this information gathering stuff? Rather than wasting my time on this, wouldn't it be better if I just started implementing my action plan?" Because you want to be as efficient and effective as possible in achieving your career advancement goals, these are important questions to ask.

When my clients think about skipping this resource-list activity, I often talk to them about how much more work it is to find a needle in a haystack. You're not sure where to look. Compare that to having a treasure map that shows you exactly where to look to find the prize you seek.

Creating a resource list of people and places is like developing your very own customized treasure map. Sure, it takes some effort, but the time and frustration it will save you is immeasurable. Plus it's likely that as you begin to research organizations and contacts, your career advancement options and goals will expand into areas you'd never considered before—and, potentially, you'll uncover possibilities that will be even more appealing to you.

Career Champ Profile: Alex

Alex's career advancement goal was to move up one level in his career and land a position as director of manufacturing with a low- to mid-tech company. For months, he scoured the postings listed on the major online sites, and submitted his resume for any positions that met his career-progress criteria. He applied for jobs across the nation, from Philly to San Francisco, from Miami to Minneapolis, and each week got more frustrated with the process. "I feel so scattered," he confessed to me during a career counseling session one day. "Sure, I can most likely land one of these jobs, but do I really want to live in Akron, if that's where I receive an offer?"

Rather than continuing to search countrywide, I recommended that Alex pick a few areas of the country where he'd prefer to live, and then research a list of target companies that fit his career advancement criteria. He knew exactly where he wanted to live and work: "My wife and I have always wanted to be in the Portland, Oregon, area—either that or stay in Colorado, either north or near Colorado Springs."

For his homework, I asked Alex to research low- to mid-tech businesses located in his ideal geographic locations. "Don't worry whether or not they're hiring now," I suggested, "just create a list." Over the next month, Alex developed a database of about 100 companies, and sent a resume and a letter of introduction to the president or VP of manufacturing at each company. "This feels more efficient and focused," Alex told me during one of our sessions.

A few weeks later, Alex received a request to interview for a director of manufacturing position with a metals producer just outside Portland. The interview resulted in an attractive offer, and Alex and his wife moved a month later. Alex had achieved his career advancement goal, which was made even more rewarding because he'd targeted—and landed—a job in his dream city.

Core Courage Concept

Career Cowards often worry that if they dig more deeply into their plans—such as by creating a list of target companies and contacts—they'll discover that what they want really isn't possible after all. Not knowing almost seems a better alternative. Yet what if the opposite was true (and I've seen over and over that it is)—that by gathering information, you'd unearth even more options than you ever imagined? So your choices are to stay in an unhappy state of ignorance, worrying that your possibilities are slim to none, or to do a little research, and see what you might find. I vote that you go for it!

Confidence Checklist

- ☐ Determine individuals and businesses you need to know.
- ☐ Create a resource database.

Chapter 5

Get Involved in Career-Advancing Associations, Clubs, and Groups

Remember the first time you were part of a team that accomplished something impressive? Now think about what it would have been like to work through that project solo. Having a team working toward a goal is typically more powerful. This same concept applies to career progress. When you connect yourself with the right groups and associations, you can move forward faster and more easily—especially in the area of career progress. The challenge is to find the right groups to meet your needs, and this chapter will show you how.

Risk It or Run From It?

- **Risk Rating:** Low to medium. For Career Cowards who get nervous meeting new people, some of the suggestions in this chapter might seem a little intimidating.

- **Payoff Potential:** Pretty impressive. Observing the results of my clients over the years, participation in associations and organizations consistently leads to speedy progress, as well as

(continued)

(continued)

access to the highest quality career advancement resources available.

- **Time to Complete:** About 15 minutes to brainstorm and locate some organizations. A few hours to actually check out one or more of them.

- **Bailout Strategy:** Groups and associations are just some of the resources that can support your CAP. If joining one or more groups doesn't appeal to you, skip over this chapter and choose activities from the other chapters that are a better fit for your style.

- **The "20 Percent Extra" Edge:** Connecting yourself with other (possibly more experienced) experts in your fields of interest can quickly skyrocket your opportunities and knowledge.

- **"Go For It!" Bonus Activity:** As you research potential professional groups, see if you can also uncover information about their annual international or national conferences, and considering adding attendance at one of these conferences to your CAP.

How to Hook into Groups That Will Support Your Progress

From quilters to accountants, project managers to beekeepers, a group exists for practically every profession or personal interest you can imagine. In the next few pages, you'll find out how to uncover and connect with clubs and associations that can put muscle behind making your CAP a reality.

Consider Which Types of Groups Will Best Meet Your Needs

Review your CAP from chapter 3, as well as your resource list from chapter 4, and ask yourself, "To achieve what I want, who do I want to connect with and what groups are they likely to be a part of?" If you want to progress in your current line of work, you'll want to find groups made up of people from your present specialty or industry. If you want to start or grow a business, you'll want to connect with individuals who can offer support and referrals. And if you're looking to create more balance in your life, involvement in civic or nonprofit organizations might be the right path for you.

Here are several types of groups to consider, along with the key advantages offered by each:

- **Civic organizations:** These groups are locally based and focus on improving the community through a variety of volunteer and fund-raising activities (think Rotary and Junior League). Become active in one of these groups, and you'll have the opportunity to rub elbows with successful, motivated humanitarians from a wide range of industries and specialties within your community.

  - *Key Advantage:* Civic organizations can be especially helpful to you if one of your career advancement aims is to connect with a range of local business leaders.

- **Business networking and mastermind groups:** You're most likely familiar with chamber of commerce organizations and business networking groups, such as BNI (Business Networking International). These entities are designed to help area businesspeople network with each other regularly, to provide support and referrals.

  Another type of support group to consider is a mastermind group. In the early 1900s, Napoleon Hill introduced the concept of the mastermind group—a gathering of a small number of people tasked with providing ideas and support to others for the purpose of goal achievement. Mastermind group formats vary, from one individual being the ongoing focus of the group, to all the group members alternating sharing the focus.

For instance, one real-estate specialist I know handpicked a number of smart, successful individuals, each with expertise in an area important to his career advancement goals, to provide him guidance. Once each quarter he treats them to dinner at a nice restaurant, and picks their brains for advice on a variety of topics. Year to year, his success has grown, largely due to the excellent guidance he's received from his mastermind team. Compiling your own group of experts might provide you with an effective resource for ideas and support.

- *Key advantage:* Mastermind groups can help you really dig in on finding ways to achieve a specific career goal. Your time spent with a mastermind group will be intense, with less socializing and involvement in community-focused activities.

- **Hobby clubs and nonprofit organizations:** Like to hike? Want to protect your local rivers? Have strong beliefs around a certain political affiliation or religion? As a way to connect with others and make progress toward your goals, consider becoming a part of a group whose main focus is around a topic you feel passionately about. Your love for knitting could be instrumental in your career advancement.

For instance, Sam, a professional organizer, regularly serves on boards and committees at her church. Through these activities, her team members get to see her organizational skills in action, and she's landed many new clients this way.

- *Key advantage:* Hobby and social groups can be some of the most comfortable to join. Because you share a passion for a topic, an instant connection between you and others already exists. So rather than trying to find things in common to build a relationship, you already have a head start.

- **Professional associations:** Just pick up a tube of toothpaste to find an example of a professional association—the American Dental Association (ADA). Hundreds of thousands of professional groups exist worldwide, and chances are there are several connected to your career focus. Sometimes they're aligned along your specialty itself, such as the Northern Colorado Writers Association, or they might be connected to the industry you're a part of, such as the International Hotel and Restaurant Association.

Professional associations range from huge, global entities with members who gather for international conferences each year to very small groups such as four accountants who meet once each month at a local breakfast spot to compare client experiences. Many allow you to participate on different levels. For instance, my father is active in the Liquid Propane Gas Association, and he attends national, regional, and local meetings to help him advance his career interests while supporting others.

- *Key advantage:* If you're looking to climb the ladder within your current career, professional groups will provide you with the most concentrated access to colleagues who might be able to help you open new doors.

Panic Point! Does the idea of connecting with others through any kind of group seem terrifying or unpleasant to you? Would you rather schedule a root canal than schmooze at a business after-hours event? If so, no worries. The groups described in this chapter are just *some* examples of resources available to you to support your career advancement. If you're reluctant to connect with others face to face, then you might want to seek out organizations with online chat rooms or telephone- or Web-based meetings. You don't have to be a "joiner" to get ahead (although it certainly can help). If flying solo is more your style, keep reading. There are many more advancement options available to you that don't require you to get involved in a group.

Locate Actual Groups to Investigate

To locate a few of these groups to consider, visit your favorite search engine and input keywords connected to your career goals. For instance, let's say that you live in Phoenix, Arizona, and you want to find a few groups to help support your CAP of starting a sideline business baking cupcakes for local coffee shops, convenience stores, and restaurants. Working within the categories described in the preceding section, I used Google to uncover the following possible organizations:

- **Civic organizations:** The Phoenix Rotary 100 or Junior League of Phoenix would help you meet other area business leaders.

- **Business networking and mastermind groups:** Another option is to investigate joining the Greater Phoenix Chamber of Commerce or the Business Networking International Northwest Valley Phoenix chapter.

- **Hobby clubs and nonprofit organizations:** Since you love to make your cupcakes look beautiful, you might want to investigate the International Cake Exploration Society (ICES), which meets in Phoenix once each month, or the Westside Cake Club, an affiliate of ICES. And since you're also a passionate supporter of improving literacy among children, you might want to check out All-Star Kids, a nonprofit volunteer tutoring organization.

- **Professional associations:** Although there's an American Bakers Association, I wasn't able to find an Arizona or Phoenix chapter using the Internet. However, I was able to locate an Arizona Hospitality and Restaurant Association, which has a variety of activities and members in the Phoenix area. From a convenience store angle, you might also want to consider the Petroleum Marketers Association of Arizona. (Hey, maybe you'll meet my dad sometime!)

As you can see, in just a few minutes, I was able to uncover nine groups to consider, using a search engine on the Internet and inputting keywords connected to career goals. If you try this process and find that it's not working well for you, call or stop by the reference desk at your local library and ask for their assistance in identifying relevant organizations. For additional ideas, you can also ask colleagues and instructors which groups they belong to.

Evaluate Great Fits and Steer Clear of Mismatches

Once you find some groups to consider, investigate them more closely through the following activities:

- **Check out their Web page and surf for articles.** The BNI Northwest Valley Chapter Web site, for instance, states that the group meets every Wednesday at noon. They have about 20 members from a wide variety of business specialties, and their primary purpose is to generate business referrals.

- **Contact the organizer or membership chair to ask about the group.** The Westside Cake Club lists a contact name and e-mail address for anyone interested in learning more about the group. A quick e-mail saying, "I'm interested in improving my decorating skills and in finding ways to build a business producing and selling cupcakes in the Phoenix area. Do you think I might be a good fit for your group?" would allow you to find out more.

- **Attend a meeting, just for fun.** The Greater Phoenix Chamber of Commerce Web site lists several upcoming Business for Breakfast, Professional Women's Roundtable, and After 5 Mixer events. Pick one and plan to go. Most organizations invite prospective members to attend a meeting or two to check out the group. Don't put pressure on yourself to meet several people right away. Instead, feel free to hang back a little to observe what's going on. Do aim to talk with one or two people about their involvement in the group and what they've gotten out of it so far. Ideally, it's best to attend at least two meetings before making a decision to join, because the first meeting might just seem overwhelming. At the second meeting, you'll have a better idea about what to expect, and you'll be able to absorb more relevant information to help with your decision making.

Through these baby steps, you can check out a group slowly to make sure it's the right fit for you before diving in with both feet.

Get Involved and Grow—or Give It Up and Move On

When you do find a group or two you want to join, make it a priority to participate actively. At the very least, aim to attend the majority of the meetings, and especially attend any annual conferences offered, where the best of the best gather to exchange information and support. If at all possible, become active on a project or committee, where you'll have the opportunity to get to know others while building important skills.

If you find after a while that the group isn't helping you toward achievement of your career advancement goals, double check that you've truly given yourself the opportunity to become involved. As with most things in life, you get out of it what you put in. And if you truly have given the group a fair shot, feel free to set your participation aside for a while to try out other groups.

Why It's Worth Doing

Being among like-minded people can be a motivating and affirming experience. Years ago I attended a two-week training course led by Richard Bolles, author of *What Color Is Your Parachute?*. In the opening session, I had a chance to talk with other group members about why they'd signed up for the course. In just a few minutes, I discovered that for most of the people in the group—other career counselors like myself—our goals were very similar: We wanted to add more skills and expertise to our toolboxes, to be able to better support our clients. I also learned that many of our values were very similar. It was as if I'd landed on a planet of people very similar to myself, and it was incredibly exciting.

Finding the right professional affiliation—whether it's a group of four other business owners who meet once each month over coffee to share their recent trials and triumphs, or a 50,000-member association with its own headquarters and national conferences—can help you achieve your career advancement goals and keep you motivated to progress day after day.

Career Champ Profile: Melia

Melia's career advancement plan included making more connections with colleagues to help her grow her freelance resume-writing business. After scoping out a variety of professional groups, she located the National Resume Writers' Association and signed up to attend their annual conference in California.

On the first day of the four-day event, Melia made a connection that could lead to additional resume-writing work; she talked with a national recruiting firm that was exhibiting at the conference looking for qualified resume writers to prepare resumes for their candidates. Melia interviewed with a representative and established herself with the company as a freelance writer, allowing her to move forward on one of her career advancement goals—plus, she had an excellent experience at the conference overall!

Core Courage Concept

Taking the risk to find and connect with others can seem terrifying, especially to Career Cowards. What if you don't like them—and worse, what if they don't like you? Rejection is a horrible feeling. Yet to be fair, we also need to consider the flip side: When you build relationships with others toward meaningful goals, and you're all benefiting, it's one of the best feelings in the world. Taking baby steps to find and investigate the right groups for you allows you to minimize your risks, while still keeping yourself open to reaping the career advancement rewards you want to achieve. C'mon, keep tiptoeing forward. You can do it!

Confidence Checklist

☐ Consider which types of groups will best meet your needs.

☐ Locate actual groups to investigate.

☐ Evaluate great fits and steer clear of mismatches.

☐ Get involved and grow…or give it up and move on.

Chapter 6

Make Progress Through Other People

When we hear the word *networking*, most of us picture someone brownnosing with higher ups in an effort to schmooze his or her way (often unfairly) into opportunities. "That's just not my style," you might argue. "I want to be sincere, not manipulative. Networking with others to get ahead just isn't for me." Hey, I'm with you on this one! Faking interest and kindness in hopes of landing a plum opportunity just doesn't seem right.

Yet you probably understand, deep down, that when done right, networking can be a highly powerful and advantageous process. In this section, I'll describe techniques for connecting with others in ways that will feel more sincere and comfortable to you. These approaches can lead to mutually beneficial results, and they don't require you to pretend you're someone you're not. These techniques can help speed up your career advancement process, and chances are they might even turn out to be fun, too!

Risk It or Run From It?

- **Risk Rating:** Mid to high risk rating for this one, especially if the idea of networking feels uncomfortable to you.

(continued)

(continued)

- **Payoff Potential:** Although you might hate the idea of networking, you're probably acutely aware of how powerful this career advancement technique can be.

- **Time to Complete:** Networking conversations typically take a few minutes to set up, and up to an hour or so to execute.

- **Bailout Strategy:** There are several career advancement strategies described in this book. If connecting with others for networking just won't work for you, check out the other techniques to find a few that are more in line with your style.

- **The "20 Percent Extra" Edge:** Nudging yourself out of your comfort zone to connect with new people will keep you green and growing, rather than stuck and stagnant. Most people are nervous about meeting new people, but if you don't let that stop you, you'll make better overall progress on your CAP.

- **"Go For It!" Bonus Activity:** Create a list of influential contacts in your field that you'd love to connect with. These people can serve as "stretch-contacts" for you as you build your networking skills.

How to Connect with Others for Career Advancement Success

Moving ahead almost always requires establishing meaningful connections with people who are able to support you in achieving your goals, just as you support them. The following easy steps will help you decide with whom you want to begin growing your network, as well as provide a proven process for successful networking interactions.

Prioritize Your People Connections

In chapter 4, you created a resource list of individuals (or at least types of people you'd like to connect with) who would be directly involved in making it possible for you to achieve your career progress goals. Even though this starter list might not be as comprehensive as you'd like it to be, pull it out now and review your initial ideas. Having just one or two people in mind is enough to help you get started. I'll show you how to take your small starter list and evolve it into a powerful career-progress resource. Also review your CAP from chapter 3 and ask yourself, "Who on this list would be helpful to talk with about my career progress goals?"

Then, just for fun, choose one person from your list and make some notes about what you'd like to discuss with this person. By listing a few potential topics, it's likely that your motivation for following through will take a tiny leap upward. From there, you can phone or e-mail that person with this request:

> I'm working toward achieving some career goals, and I'd like to talk with you to brainstorm some next steps. Would you be willing to meet me for coffee or talk with me on the phone sometime in the next few weeks?

Panic Point! Are you looking at your list and thinking either a) I have absolutely no one to put on my list, or b) of the people I've listed, none of these individuals would be able to help me? If this sounds like you, you're not alone. In fact, most of the thousands of clients I've worked with have had this initial reaction. You might believe that if people in your network could truly assist your progress, they would have already, right? Well, there's one significant flaw in this argument: If you haven't shared your *specific* career goals with these individuals, they wouldn't have known how to help you, even if they wanted to. So don't discount your existing contacts too hastily.

If you have absolutely *no one* on your list, reconsider former coworkers, classmates, teachers—even your insurance representative or real-estate agent. Keep in mind that these people don't need to hire you for an opportunity; rather, their primary purpose will be to help you expand your list of contacts and possibilities, bringing

(continued)

(continued)

> you closer to your goals. So ask yourself again if there's anybody—even one person—that you could list. If not, consider hooking up with a professional association, as described in chapter 5, and attempting to network with one of the board members.

Master People-Connecting Basics

Once you've set up a time to connect with one of your contacts, prepare yourself for a successful conversation. I recommend sticking with a foolproof agenda that will lead to win-win results for both you and your contacts. This approach, one that I call "You, Me, We," provides step-by-step details for what to say and when to say it. This concept originally came from job search expert Daniel Porot as an outline for cover letters. I've adapted it as a highly effective agenda for career advancement brainstorming conversations.

To show you how it works, imagine that you (we'll call you Chris for this example) want to land a position one level up within your current company, and you have arranged to meet Kelly for coffee. She's a colleague who works for your same employer, but in a different division. Your conversation will follow this basic outline:

- **You:** In this initial part of the meeting, you will focus on Kelly, as in "Kelly, I am going to first to focus on *you.*" (That's where the "you" pronoun comes in.) This part of the meeting should take somewhere between 5 and 10 minutes.

- **Me:** In the second part of the meeting, shift the focus back to yourself, as in, "Now I'm going to spend a few minutes talking about what's going on with *me.*" This will take you five minutes or less.

- **We:** In this last part of the conversation, you and Kelly will be brainstorming together—that's the "we" part. This segment should take five minutes or less.

Now that we have the pronouns straight (You = Kelly, Me = Chris, We = Kelly and Chris together), I'll cover these sections in more detail.

The "You" Part of the Conversation

The purpose of the "You" segment in the agenda is to connect with your contact in a meaningful way and to get the conversation off to a good start. By focusing first on Kelly, you show her that she's important to you, and you increase your chances of her supporting you later in the conversation. My favorite "You" focus strategy is the FORD technique, an acronym standing for Family, Occupation, Recreation, and Dreams. Asking questions about these topics allows you to focus successfully on your contact. Here are some examples:

- **Family:** "Where are you from originally? Do you have family in this area?"

- **Occupation:** "Tell me how things are going for you in your work. What aspects of your job are particularly exciting or challenging for you right now?"

- **Recreation:** "What do you do for fun? Have you been on any interesting trips or vacations recently?"

- **Dreams:** "Where do you hope to take things in the future? Are there any exciting projects or developments that you're aiming for?"

Feel free to modify the FORD questions to come up with some that feel comfortable to you. And realize that you don't need to ask your contact about *every* topic within the FORD acronym—it's just a handy memory technique to help you keep the conversation going smoothly. And believe me, it *will* go smoothly, provided that you ask good questions and then *listen* to Kelly's responses. Here are a few tips to ensure that you're listening successfully:

- **Make eye contact** (however, it's perfectly fine to shift your eyes away from Kelly occasionally—you don't want her to feel like you're glaring at her). If you're uncomfortable looking directly at Kelly, look at the space between her eyes instead.

- **Truly focus on what's being said.** One of the biggest mistakes people make in conversing with others is thinking about how they're going to respond before the other person has even finished talking. Don't *worry* about what you're going to say next, and instead listen intently to Kelly. Chances are very good that as you listen, you'll come up with another question to ask her, allowing you to keep the conversation going. And if there's a little pause in the conversation, while you think of your next question, that's okay, too.

- **Avoid jumping in with your own "stuff."** It's so tempting to want to share your own experiences when talking with someone else, as in, "Oh, I once had a dog, too!" Remember, the first part of this conversation is about *Kelly*, so keep the focus on her. Your turn will come shortly.

After you've spent 5 to 10 minutes learning about Kelly and what's going on in her life, you'll then need to move into the "Me" part of the conversation. A good way to segue this transition is to look at your timepiece (your watch, your cell phone, the clock on the wall) and say:

> Kelly, I want to be sure that I make good use of your time, so I'm going to now tell you a little bit about what's going on with me....

This is a *very* handy statement to master, because otherwise you might end up spending the entire conversation on the "You" part of the agenda, and never get to the "Me" and "We" segments.

The "Me" Part of the Conversation

So let's say you've just spent the last 5 to 10 minutes catching up on Kelly's life. Now it's time to move into the "Me" part of the agenda to bring Kelly up to speed on what's going on with you and your career advancement activities.

Panic Point! Nervous about putting the focus on yourself for fear that you'll come across as self-centered? Again, this is a *very* typical Career Coward fear. But keep in mind that you've just focused intently on your contact for 5 to 10 minutes, so now it's *your* turn, and your contact is *expecting* you to talk about your job search, because you mentioned it when you set up the meeting. Plus, you'll be keeping this part of the conversation to 5 minutes or less, so it will be over before you know it.

In the "Me" part of your conversation, you want to aim to cover two points:

- Clearly state your career advancement goal, as in "I'm looking to move up to the next level in my project management career, ideally overseeing a project with both domestic and international components."

- Briefly state a few highlights of your background* that are related to your career advancement goal, and share a current resume if it's appropriate. For instance you might say, "Kelly, in my current position, I manage computer development projects with budgets of up to $5 million. I've been very successful in this job, consistently completing projects on time or ahead of time, as well as under budget." Your goal with this activity is to paint a picture for Kelly about what you're great at and what you want to do more of in the future, using one to two specific examples from your past.

    *If you need additional ideas about how to describe a few key pieces of your background, check out **The Career Coward's Guide to Interviewing** for suggestions.

Once you cover these two "Me" pieces, then you can transition to the last part of the conversation—the "We" piece. A smooth way to move into this portion of the agenda is to say:

> Now that you know a little about what I'm aiming to do, I'd love to brainstorm some next steps with you....

The "We" Part of the Conversation

You're in the home stretch now! Now you just need to wrap up your conversation with a successful "We" discussion. Here's how this part of the conversation goes:

1. Pull out two copies of a streamlined version of your resource list (the one you developed in chapter 4, listing people, departments, organizations, and companies that could help you make progress toward your career goals; for networking purposes, you only need to list people and company names, not addresses, contact info, and so on). Hand one to Kelly, and say, "I'd like to get your input on the following people and organizations I'm researching."

2. Ask, "What do you know about any of these people and businesses on my list—pros and cons, updates about what's happening with them, people I should talk to, and so on?"

3. Listen and make notes as Kelly offers some thoughts. For instance, she might say, "Well, XYZ division just landed a huge computer development contract that includes working with offices in South America and Africa. I have a friend, Bill, who is a friend of the division vice president. Oh, and ABC division is supposedly going to expand their operations soon, opening an office in London. My friend Meg works in that group. I'd recommend staying away from LMNOP division. I hear the VP there is a bear to work under." As she's talking, show interest, but resist the urge to "Yeah, but..." her ideas, as in "Yeah, but I'm not interested in ABC division because...." If you "Yeah, but..." Kelly's ideas, she'll want to stop offering them.

4. Ask for clarification and confirm the next steps. For instance, "Kelly, you mentioned that XYZ division just landed a huge international contract. I'd like to learn more about that. Do you have any suggestions for getting more information?" And, "You said that your friends Bill and Meg know about what's happening with some of the other divisions within the company. I'd love to talk with them. Would it be okay if I contacted them and mentioned that I talked with you?"

5. Thank her for her time, and provide her with a business card or calling card.

6. Follow up with a written (e-mail or hardcopy) thank you note within 48 hours.

7. Using the contacts you've been provided, repeat the process of requesting meetings, following the "You, Me, We" outline, and continue to grow your network.

That's it! Not *too* terrible, is it? And now that you know how these "You, Me, We" conversations work, keep reading to find out how you can keep your connections moving forward successfully.

Make the Most of Mentoring Moments

The minute I saw the fairy godmother appear in the movie *Cinderella*, I knew I wanted one of my own—someone who had my best interests at heart and who could make magical, wonderful things happen for me. Many of us wish for a similar fairy godmother resource in our careers: a person who recognizes our potential, guides us in making good choices, and opens doors to opportunities along the way.

While fairy godmothers can be hard to come by, mentors—or at least people who are able to provide us with mentoring moments—can be discovered and cultivated. You might already have a mentor or two in your life, someone you've known for a while who is able to provide important career guidance when you need it most. If you're lucky enough to have access to this kind of resource, treat this person as a precious gem, because effective mentors can be hard to find.

If you don't have a mentor, consider taking advantage of "mentoring moments" that might pop up with people you connect with along the way: coworkers, bosses, colleagues, instructors, and others. This is a concept I learned from organizational development consultant Ava Diamond. Rather than putting pressure on yourself to create a formal, intimate mentoring relationship with just one individual, instead recognize that everyone has the potential to share a pearl or two of wisdom with you. At the right moment, you can ask a contact a strategic question or two to support your career advancement efforts. The following are sample questions you might ask a networking contact:

- If you were in my shoes, trying to accomplish the career goals I've described, what would you do?

- Did you ever find yourself in a situation similar to mine, and if so, what did you do?

- Now that you know a little about me and what I'm looking to accomplish, what other thoughts or ideas do you have that I should consider?

- What are a few of the guiding principles that have helped you to achieve successful results in your career?

The feedback you receive could be the key that unlocks the door to your next valuable career opportunity.

Infuse Your Network with Internet Power

In addition to your face-to-face networking efforts, you might also want to take advantage of online networking tools such as LinkedIn (www.linkedin.com). LinkedIn allows you to create an electronic record of contacts in your network. Others can connect to you to share relevant job openings and business development opportunities, and you can support others with connections and information as they progress in their careers. There are many ways to control and benefit from the connections on LinkedIn, and chances are, it would be a valuable resource for you.

Facebook (www.facebook.com), an online social networking tool, might also be helpful. This resource allows you to create a unique, visual, and interactive profile of who you are as a person. So when others want to learn about you—recruiters, potential customers, and so on—they could access Facebook to learn more.

All online networking tools have their advantages and disadvantages, so do your homework before jumping in. But keep in mind that if you're looking to grow your network, the more tools you have to work with, the more you'll be able to achieve the results you want.

Why It's Worth Doing

In their hearts, most people know that if they would connect more with others, they'd be able to make better progress toward their career goals. Yet knowing that it makes sense to take a step and actually doing it are two very different challenges.

If, in the past, you haven't actively connected with others toward achieving your career goals, it's likely that this activity will feel awkward. Just like riding a bike, it takes practice to learn how to do it successfully. Yet think about your career goals from a longer-term perspective. Imagine it's five years from now and you've successfully achieved your CAP. Imagine that as part of this success, you've had to learn how to network with others to build relationships and uncover opportunities. As you picture your future self, how does it feel knowing that you're now a capable networker, capable of achieving even greater successes in the future?

Chances are that as you look at your life from this longer-range view, you can see that it would be silly to let your short-term fears of networking get in the way of your long-term career successes. After a few networking conversations, you'll most likely be saying to yourself, "What was I so afraid of anyway?"

Career Champ Profile: Tilly

Tilly was adamant about not networking. "It's so fake!" she told me emphatically during one of our meetings. A few months earlier, she'd defined her career advancement goal as moving into a new division within her company that was planning and executing international conferences to help wipe out poverty worldwide. This career focus was highly interesting to her, yet she didn't want to have to "brown-nose" to land a position in the division.

"Just try one networking conversation, to humor me," I pleaded with her. Her CAP could offer so much value to the world, and I wanted to see her succeed. "Just one…" Tilly sighed heavily. "Okay. Recently I sat in a meeting with one of the VPs in the new division. During the coffee break we spoke for a minute. I could follow up with her to brainstorm some next steps using your 'You, Me, We' outline. I'll give it a chance, just to humor you."

About a week later, Tilly called me. "Oh my gosh!" she gushed in her phone message to me. "That conversation was so helpful! The VP gave me a referral to the head of the division. She also said they were planning to add staff in the next few months."

Over the next few weeks, Tilly became an enthusiastic networker, meeting with several individuals in the division. She sent me an e-mail about two months later. "I just landed a job in the new division, and I'm now in charge of organizing a major international conference on poverty. You were right; the contacts I made were so important to making my career goal a reality. I'm a convert!"

Core Courage Concept

Meeting new people, sharing your goals and ideas, and asking for input and support can seem overwhelming, especially if you haven't had much experience with networking. (What if you're rejected or come across looking like a fool?) Yet the rewards can far outweigh the risks, especially when you consider that the knowledge and backing of others can multiply your ability to achieve your career advancement objectives. Begin with just one, follow a proven process, and allow networking to help you truly succeed.

Confidence Checklist

- ☐ Prioritize your people connections.
- ☐ Master people-connecting basics.
- ☐ Make the most of mentoring moments.
- ☐ Infuse your network with Internet power.

Chapter 7

Find and Choose Training That's "Just Right" for You

Training programs today are so varied the choices can seem overwhelming. There are online degree programs, self-paced instructional DVDs, hands-on learning with an expert, skill-building courses at conferences and community colleges, and more. Because there are literally millions of possibilities for education and learning, having a step-by-step process for evaluating your options will save you from wasting valuable time, effort, and expense, and put you on a faster track for achieving your career advancement successes.

Risk It or Run From It?

- **Risk Rating:** Because education can require a significant investment of time, energy, and money, there's medium risk associated with choosing and completing a training program.

- **Payoff Potential:** Excellent! Fill in holes in your training, and your success can skyrocket.

- **Time to Complete:** A few hours to a number of years, depending on the training you need to support your career goals.

(continued)

(continued)

- **Bailout Strategy:** Additional education isn't necessary in every career advancement scenario. Do some research to determine if additional education is even required for achieving your CAP.

- **The "20 Percent Extra" Edge:** Investing in your training will help you stay more marketable and motivated throughout your career.

- **"Go For It!" Bonus Activity:** For fun, research the top people in your chosen line of work, and read their bios to determine their training credentials. The choices they've made might help guide your own educational plans.

How to Uncover and Evaluate Training Possibilities

By keeping your career advancement objective in mind as you evaluate the wide range of training possibilities available, you'll be able to uncover and choose the educational options that are just right for you.

Be Clear on Your Career Progress Goal

Many talented, ambitious clients have begun our work together by telling me, "I think I need to go back to school for another degree." I usually respond with: "What program are you considering, and how will you use it?" A typical reply is, "Well, I don't really know. It's just that I feel stuck in my career, and I figured a new degree would jump-start things."

In my career counselor role, I've also heard as many (or more) people say, "Well, I've gotten this degree, but now I'm not sure what to do with it." While additional education can definitely open new doors, simply completing a degree doesn't offer any guarantee of advancement. In fact, the time, energy, and money it costs to obtain formal education might even land you in a frustrating financial hole that leaves you feeling more stuck than before. So be wary of viewing more education as a fix-all for blocked career progress. As you think about obtaining more education—either through a formal or informal avenue—choose training that will support your overall plan, rather than have your plan solely be to get more education.

As a reminder of where you're aiming to go, reread the initial CAP you created in chapter 3. Ask yourself, "How can additional education help me achieve the objectives I've set for myself?" For instance, in my plan I listed my overall goal as:

> I want to keep progressing in my current line of work. I want to grow my career counseling practice, helping more clients through activities that help them achieve their career goals more effectively and successfully. I also want to keep developing myself within the field of career counseling, improving my credentials and knowledge.

And a specific action item I listed was:

> Increase the financial value of what I have to offer the world by investing in myself with further education—maybe a Ph.D.

These two components of my plan give me some specific educational objectives to consider and work toward.

Analyze Educational Qualifications Necessary to Achieve Your Objective

If your plan does call for more training, take the time to determine exactly which types of education will best support your career goal. Ideally, you want the level of training you receive to match the requirements of your goals as closely as possible, without leaving you over- or underqualified—or over- or underprepared. The following activities can help you quickly and easily determine the level of education most ideal for your career goal:

- **Look at job descriptions:** If you're looking to move up in your career, review a number of job descriptions for the type of position you'd ultimately like to land. A quick search on popular job sites, such as www.monster.com or www.jobfox.com, should provide you with easy access to job descriptions and the requirements listed for those positions. Create a listing of the educational requirements included, and chances are you'll notice a trend fairly quickly.

- **Do a survey:** Another effective exercise for determining ideal educational credentials is to conduct a quick survey with others already involved in those roles to find out what kind of training they've received. Ask questions such as, "Ultimately I'd like to be in a position similar to the one you're in now. What type of training is typically required, and what are your recommendations for obtaining it?"

- **Find out what you lack:** If it's your goal to modify your existing work, to make it a better fit for you, what else do you need to know to propose and succeed with your ideal plan? Perhaps you'll need to improve in a particular skill or knowledge area. What training would provide you with the new expertise you'll need? It might be taking a one-semester course or training with a coworker to learn a new process.

To the best of your ability, identify the holes you might have in your education as they relate to your career goals. Then determine which training avenues will equip you with the expertise you need.

Investigate Several Avenues for Learning

When we hear the word "education," most of us immediately think of formal training programs offered by brick-and-mortar colleges and universities. Yet avenues for gaining the skills you need are now so diverse that you don't need to be confined to traditional learning programs. Consider the many options described here as possibilities for obtaining the training you need, and use Internet search engines to locate specific education programs.

- **Formal degree and certificate programs:** In some situations, a formal degree or certificate is a required credential to achieve your career goal. To move ahead in many career-track positions, for example, a minimum of a bachelor's degree is required. For professions such as accounting, architecture, medicine, and law, a degree and licensure are essential.

If you find your career progress blocked by a lack of a degree, license, or certificate, you might need to invest the time, energy, and funds to earn the required credential. Keep in mind, however, that training options today are highly flexible, allowing you to take online or self-paced courses, and making it possible to more easily fit your education into your existing routine. And in many cases, as soon as you begin your training, new doors of opportunity will open for you, even it if takes you years to receive the actual credential.

Panic Point! Many people freak out over the prospect of having to complete a multiyear degree program, and instead of committing to this big step, they attempt to sidestep it by taking numerous, shorter-term, skill-building workshops and classes. I've seen this come up many times with clients who truly need to complete a bachelor's degree to move forward. "Maybe these professional development courses will suffice," they hope. But in certain situations, a degree is the *only* credential that will allow you to keep progressing in your career. Rather than delaying your success further, consider taking just one course toward your degree, and tell yourself, "I can stop at any time if I decide to." Chances are you'll discover that with enough time and effort, you'll be able to complete the degree you need, and you'll actually like doing it, because it's focused on topics that are interesting to you.

- **Skill-building courses:** It could be that a full-fledged degree or certificate program is overkill for your training needs. If this is the case, check into skill-building classes offered through professional associations, community colleges, and organizations such as your local Small Business Development Center. In exchange for a reasonable course fee and the investment of a few hours of your time, you could successfully prepare yourself for the next step on your career path.

- **On-the-job training:** Perhaps you're already equipped with most of what you need to know to keep moving forward, except for a particular process or a few techniques that you could learn on the job or through the guidance of a mentor or co-worker. Obtain an okay from your boss to cross-train with a colleague who possesses the knowledge you need, even if it's after hours. Or offer to work for free with an expert to learn a skill in exchange for the support you provide to them in another area (see chapter 9 for more details on this avenue).

- **Self-instruction:** In some cases, you can acquire the expertise you need on your own, either by reading a few books on the subject, or training yourself using instructional DVD or audio programs. Many of the most successful individuals in the world today taught themselves everything they needed to know.

Ask for Advice from Experts

Before you jump with both feet into any training program you're considering, run your plan by an expert or two who are experienced in your desired line of work. Describe your proposed training plan, and ask for their opinions on its appropriateness for your situation.

If you're not sure who to ask for advice, research a professional association tied to your career goal and contact one or more of the board members with your questions (review chapter 5 for more details on finding and connecting with professional groups). Their input can help you avoid wasting time and money, and steer you in a direction that will support your long-term career advancement success.

Why It's Worth Doing

It's true; the right kind of education—or lack of it—can make (or break) your career progress. Yet locating a training option that fits your needs without draining you of too much time and money can be tricky. Determining what makes sense for your situation can help you succeed with your career advancement goals quicker and more easily.

For instance, I once considered opening a business sewing furniture slipcovers. My grandmother had owned a business like this, and it seemed to be a good fit for my interests and lifestyle goals. One little hitch was that I didn't know how to sew slipcovers, so I'd need to learn somehow, before I could begin my new venture. I checked into a variety of programs, from bachelor's degrees in home economics and textiles that would take me years and thousands of dollars to complete, to multi-DVD training programs that I could watch at home and that cost a few hundred dollars.

After weighing the possibilities for a while, I ended up contacting an experienced slipcover specialist to ask her opinion. She discouraged me from taking a structured training program. "Customers don't ask about your training or credentials," she told me. "Mostly they just want to know that you can do a nice job for them. If you have an example of your work at your studio, that's usually sufficient. Rather than a formal training course, you'd do better to learn hands on." She then offered to spend a little time showing me the basics. Because I already knew how to sew pretty well, she thought that would be sufficient.

We spent a few hours together one Saturday afternoon, I paid her $100 for her time, and I walked out with what I needed to know to begin a slipcover business. Ultimately I changed my mind about moving forward on that idea, but to this day I'm so grateful to that specialist for discouraging me from investing in a more formal training program. It saved me hundreds of hours of my time, as well as thousands of dollars in expense.

Investing a little effort on the front end researching which kind of training best suits your needs, and being open to a variety of possibilities for learning, will help you make choices that support attainment of your career advancement goals.

Career Champ Profile: Jacob

Jacob's career advancement goal was to move into the lead financial position at the engineering company where he worked within the next three years. Holly, the current chief financial officer at the company, had clearly stated that she intended to retire in the next few years, and Jacob was motivated to take over her spot.

Jacob already had a bachelor's degree in business, but he worried it wasn't enough to qualify him for the top financial spot. Holly's training included a bachelor's in accounting, plus she had her Certified Professional Accountant (CPA) credential. When we first met, Jacob was trying to decide if he needed to obtain an MBA with an emphasis in finance, complete a second bachelor's degree in accounting and then earn a CPA, or do something completely different with his education.

Over the next two months, Jacob looked into a wide range of training and degree programs by talking with advisors at schools and interviewing CFOs at different businesses. In his research, he uncovered another training possibility he hadn't known about before: earning a Certified Professional Manager (CPM) credential. It involved learning and being tested on many of the same rigorous accounting concepts required to earn a CPA, and was highly respected and accepted among top financial executives, but it didn't require Jacob to complete a bachelor's degree in accounting as a prerequisite.

Jacob decided to move ahead on earning a CPM, and he began the self-paced learning modules and standardized testing process immediately. It would take him just over two years to complete the credential. During this time, Jacob also decided to work with Holly for some additional on-the-job training toward achieving his career advancement goal of becoming a CFO.

Core Courage Concept

Because the options for education are overwhelming (not to mention the work and expense required to complete your training), it can almost seem easier to skip over this step and hope that you'll be able to realize your career goals anyway. But (heavy sigh) chances are pretty good that you'll need to enhance your knowledge base to keep moving forward. Rather than getting snowed under by all of the time and effort it will take, view the process of enhancing your training as a one-step-at-a-time project. Inch forward slowly, and before you know it, you'll have covered the miles you needed to travel.

Confidence Checklist

☐ Be clear on your career progress goal.

☐ Analyze educational qualifications necessary to achieve your objective.

☐ Investigate several avenues for learning.

☐ Ask for advice from experts.

Chapter 8

Prepare and Present Powerful Proposals

As you conduct research and connect with others, it's likely that you'll uncover some exciting possibilities: the possibility of suggesting to your boss that you should be promoted, lining up a part-time position with a company you've networked with, or preparing a proposal for a potential customer. Whatever the opportunity, the process of creating and conveying a powerful proposal can lead to exciting, career-advancing possibilities where they never existed before.

Risk It or Run From It?

- **Risk Rating:** Mid to high risk here. You'll be putting yourself on the line for a "yea" or a "nay," but...

- **Payoff Potential:** Nothing ventured, nothing gained! Yes, you might walk away with a big, fat "No," but you might also earn an enthusiastic "Let's go for it" that can change your life!

- **Time to Complete:** A few hours to create a compelling proposition; 30 minutes to deliver it.

- **Bailout Strategy:** Proposals definitely fall into the category of "Nice to do" rather than "Must do," so you can very easily skip

---

(continued)

(continued)

over this information. But before you flip to the next chapter, ask yourself, "What would it hurt for me to at least read and learn about the proposal process for when an exciting possibility does pop up?"

- **The "20 Percent Extra" Edge:** The vast majority of people wait for opportunities to come to them. Very few people define what they want and then ask for it. When you put together and present a proposal, you set yourself miles ahead of the competition.

- **"Go For It!" Bonus Activity:** Conduct a survey of successful people you know, asking them if they've ever presented a proposal. For those who have, ask for details on how they prepared and presented it, as well as suggestions for helping yours to be successful.

How to Develop and Deliver a Persuasive Proposal

In chapters 2 and 3, you defined your CAP. Since then, you've been researching resources and opportunities to achieve those goals. Along the way, it's likely that you've uncovered some exciting possibilities, a few of which may require you to make the first move. Although it may seem a little overwhelming, following the step-by-step approach will show you how to conceive and convey a powerful proposal.

Clearly Define What You Want

One of my favorite quotes is from Lewis Carroll's *Alice in Wonderland*:

One day Alice came to a fork in the road and saw a Cheshire cat in a tree. "Which road do I take?" she asked. "Where do you want to go?" was his response. "I don't know," Alice answered. "Then," said the cat, "it doesn't matter."

If you're not clear on where you want to go, there's no set path for getting there. You did, however, define your hoped-for path for career advancement and you're moving steadily toward it.

For instance, let's say that through the exercises you completed in chapter 3, you decided to branch out of your current work into some new part-time, sideline pursuits. You've decided that you want to line up an opportunity to deliver quality-improvement training sessions to manufacturing companies. This will be a separate professional activity from your regular day job, which you've decided to cut back to four days each week. You also researched and connected with two organizations that deliver these trainings, and you met for coffee with decision makers at each of those businesses. Talking with these people made you even more excited about your career advancement goal.

Faith, one of the decision makers with Quality Training Consultants, even mentioned during her meeting with you that her company is interested in adding a series of training sessions designed just for small, specialty-product manufacturers. When you heard this, bells started going off in your head because this is exactly what you love to do. You gathered some more information from her and made some mental notes about the opportunity.

Now you've decided to create a proposal for Faith, detailing how you can be a resource to her company as a quality trainer for smaller manufacturers. As a first step, you'll want to define the following:

- What activities do you want to be involved in?

- In what format do you want to execute these activities? (Full time? Part time? Partnership? Contractor?)

- How do you want to be compensated?

And let's say these are your answers to those questions:

- I want the opportunity to deliver an average of one half-day training each week to small, specialty manufacturers within an hour's drive of my home.

- I'd also like to meet with and create training proposals for the small manufacturing businesses Quality Training Consultants and I decide would be worthwhile to target, connecting with an average of two companies each week.

- I want to be compensated at $1,000 base pay each month, plus 50 percent of any trainings I sell and deliver (average training fee is $2,000 per half-day), so that ultimately, I could be earning an additional $5,000 each month in this sideline work.

Panic Point! Does the idea of detailing *exactly* what you want to do, and how you'll be paid for it, freak you out? If so, you're not alone. Many people have never experienced the process of creating a proposal specifically addressing their career goals. It's brand new to them. Plus there's the chance that their idea will be rejected (ouch). So if you're feeling a little weird about being so forward with your desires, know that you're not alone. But don't let it stop you. Tiptoe forward by actually writing up your proposal; and *then* decide whether you want to take it any further.

Good for you! You've figured out what you hope to achieve through your proposal. Now it's time to define what benefits the recipient of it will get.

Determine "What's in It for Them?"

For a proposal to be successfully considered, you'll need to show how your ideas can create a win-win opportunity for both sides. Continuing with the earlier example, you could list the benefits Faith and her company would receive for having you as part of their organization. Typically, the benefits you offer will fall into one or more of the categories in the following list. Brainstorm several potential benefits as part of your proposal-development process.

Here are some examples:

- **Make money:** Connecting with and providing training to small manufacturers could ultimately lead to an additional $36,000 in profit for Quality Training Consultants ($3,000 each month) once you're operating at full capacity.

- **Save money:** I want to work part time, so they won't need to pay a full-time employee salary or benefits. In fact, I don't even need a desk at their location. I have my own office and computer at home.

- **Improve quality:** Quality Training Consultants wants to target smaller manufacturing companies, and I'm an excellent resource to help make that happen. I have expertise in this arena and will be an outstanding, quality representative for their company.

- **Improve image:** I'm a dynamic professional who will be able to professionally represent Quality Training Consultants to about 100 smaller manufacturing companies each year. Additionally, I'll be able to deliver outstanding trainings to many of these companies, enhancing the market's knowledge of the Quality Training Consultants organization.

Your affiliation with Quality Training Consultants has the potential to deliver all of these benefits to them. Detailing what's in it for them helps you strengthen the win-win proposition.

Panic Point! What if you're not sure what's in it for them? If you're having a hard time identifying what you bring to the table, it most likely means that either you haven't yet gathered enough information to understand your target decision maker's priorities, or you may be too modest about describing your potential contributions. If you need more information about the decision maker's main concerns, line up a few more networking conversations to learn about opportunities related to your career

(continued)

(continued)

> advancement goals (see chapter 6). If you're already clear about your potential to contribute, but fuzzy on what you have to offer, challenge yourself to write down at least a few probable benefits, and then push forward to the next step. Your self belief and your understanding of the advantages you can offer are likely to grow as you progress further in the proposal-development process.

Organize Your Information for Success

You've already done the challenging work of defining what you want, as well as what's in it for the employer. Now you just need to organize your information in a professional, understandable proposal. Let's begin with the notes you've already created, plugging them into a format similar to the You, Me, We outline described in chapter 6:

- **You:** In this section, include information that will be important to the recipient of your proposal, as in, "This is what's in it for YOU."

- **Me:** Here you'll outline what you hope to achieve through the proposal, as in, "This is what's in it for ME."

- **We:** Finally, the two of you together will define what next steps you and your contact can take to move forward.

Here's a rough draft of a proposal, building off of the notes we've already created for the opportunity at Quality Training Associates. You'll see that the order has been shifted some to catch their attention with points that are of higher priority, but the content is basically the same:

You (Faith and Quality Training Associates):

- Talking with you earlier, I know that you want to expand into offering smaller manufacturing company training, and I am an excellent resource to help make that happen for you. I have expertise in this arena and would be an outstanding representative for your company.

- I possess excellent knowledge of quality processes, particularly within small manufacturing company environments, because I've worked in small-company manufacturing environments for the last 15 years, day after day. I will be able to professionally represent Quality Training Consultants to about 100 smaller manufacturing companies each year, as well as deliver outstanding trainings to many of these companies, enhancing the market's knowledge of the Quality Training Consultants organization.

- With the trainings I deliver, I can help your company earn an estimated $36,000 in profit each year.

- This would be a low-risk investment for you, as I want to work part time as a contractor without benefits. I even have my own home office and computer.

Me (what you want out of this):

- My goal would be to deliver an average of one half-day training each week to small, specialty manufacturers within an hour's drive of my home.

- I would be meeting with and creating training proposals for small manufacturing businesses that you and I decide are worthwhile to target, connecting with an average of two companies each week.

We (how do we move forward to make this happen?):

- I could begin supporting and promoting your organization immediately. I would like to be compensated at $1,000 base pay each month, plus 50 percent of any trainings I sell and deliver.

As you can see, this information could fit on a one-page document that would be easy to share with your target decision makers. Your proposal is coming together!

Practice and Present Your Proposal

You're moving into the home stretch. Your draft proposal is developed; now you just need to practice and present it. This is where things can really begin to feel scary. Take a deep breath and realize that you can take things just one inch at a time:

- **Finalize your plan:** Rework your draft until you feel solid about what you're proposing. Show it to someone you trust and ask them for input on how to make it even better.

- **Practice delivering your proposal:** Find yourself a quiet spot to talk through what you've put together. Pretend that the decision maker is at your side and act as if this is the real deal. Make notes on changes or problems you encounter during your practice and then refine your proposal further.

- **Rehearse your closing:** Practice wrapping up your proposal by saying, "What questions or concerns do you have? How can we move forward on this?"

- **Anticipate objections, rejections, and questions:** Even though your proposal may be well thought out, the decision maker may still have questions or objections that you didn't anticipate. Be open to hearing, "I need time to think about it" and "I'm not sure this would work for us," and be ready to ask further questions to learn more about their needs and hopes.

- **Schedule a conversation with the decision maker:** A request such as, "Faith, I have some ideas on how to increase Quality Training Consultants' product offerings and profitability. These are based on some thoughts you shared with me at our last meeting. Could we meet for 30 minutes to go over my proposal?" works well.

- **Deliver it and move on:** This step can seem especially overwhelming, yet I predict that once you do it, you'll feel great about yourself. If your proposal is met with a "no" or "maybe," ask questions to learn more, and then determine whether you need to revise your proposal or follow up again at a later time. Although the result may not be exactly as you expected, chances are excellent that you'll make some progress toward your career advancement goals, one way or another.

Why It's Worth Doing

On the one-year anniversary of our first date, my then-boyfriend and I were enjoying a romantic picnic in the park. One second he was happily munching on a chicken sandwich, and the next he was on one knee digging something out of his pocket. "Katrina, will you marry me?" Pete asked, sliding a twinkling diamond ring on my finger. "Yes, yes, yes!" I yelled in response, and then danced around on the grass, thrilled at what had just transpired. Pete had definitely developed and delivered a proposal that was on target: I wanted him, and he wanted me. It was an exciting win-win opportunity!

Although you might not receive as enthusiastic a response, a proposal that addresses a need or want, and that is presented in a compelling way, can lead to exhilarating results. There's risk involved, yes, but huge rewards are also a possibility.

In many cases, nothing changes until *you* get something going. A proposal offers the perfect opportunity to define what you want and present the information effectively for consideration.

Career Champ Profile: Carrie

For more than 10 years, Carrie worked in recruiting and human resources for various companies. She loved her work, yet to support her own career advancement, she wanted to find a way to do more to help others make progress in their careers. Moving toward this goal, Carrie started a sideline business helping job searchers write resumes and prepare for interviews. It was going pretty well, but after a few months, Carrie determined that she'd really rather work with a business that provided these services, so that she could collaborate on client projects instead of doing it on her own.

Carrie researched businesses in her area that provided career support services, and she networked with a few decision makers. She uncovered an exciting possibility to become an affiliate at one of those companies, and she put together the following proposal, which she mailed to me at my business, Career Solutions Group. Figure 8.1 is her proposal, which she presented to us. We were able to create a position for her.

Dear Katy,

As you plan to grow your business, I would be interested in exploring additional ways to work together. I believe that working together could complement both our services. Following is a list of activities where I possess strengths and experience that offer possibilities for us to collaborate:

- Facilitating training sessions as a marketing tool

- Delivering outstanding customer relations with an attitude of positive, nurturing support

- Coaching others to inspire and empower them

- Resume and cover letter writing

- Creating unique and effective training and development programs

- Organizing and promoting events

If you can see how any of the above would benefit Career Solutions Group, let's discuss the possibilities further. I believe we share the same goals. I would welcome the opportunity to play a more visible role in your future business plans.

Sincerely,

Carrie

Figure 8.1: Carrie's proposal.

Core Courage Concept

It takes a huge amount of courage to define what you want and then propose it to someone else. What if they say "no" and your dreams are dashed to pieces? Creating and communicating proposals can be terrifying. Yet consider this: What if you never had the chance to do the work you truly want to do? What if the only thing standing between you and your career dreams is asking the right person for the chance? From this perspective, it's even more frightening to imagine how close you could be and yet never achieve what you want. C'mon, you can do it!

Confidence Checklist

☐ Clearly define what you want.

☐ Determine "what's in it for them."

☐ Organize your information for success.

☐ Practice and present your proposal.

Chapter 9

Work for Free to Move Ahead Faster

Feel as though you've invested a ton of effort to move forward in your career, yet you keep running into brick walls? Attempted to move into positions of greater responsibility and reward with no results? Proposed to decision makers actions to take on, yet keep getting rejections? Then this might be the time to take advantage of one of the most effective career advancement tools available to you: working for free. Sometimes called an internship or practicum, working for free can help you create opportunities to advance where they never existed before. On the surface, working for free might seem impractical and even a little stupid, yet hear me out before making your final decision.

Risk It or Run From It?

- **Risk Rating:** Although there are minor risks involved in proposing to work for free (the decision maker may still say "no," even to the excellent opportunity you're offering), overall, this is a relatively low-risk activity.

- **Payoff Potential:** The reward possibilities with work-for-free arrangements are excellent. Often, doors of opportunity fly

---

(continued)

(continued)

open once you crack them just a little bit; this approach gives you the chance to get your toe in.

- **Time to Complete:** It might take just a few days to line up a work-for-free opportunity, and then a few months to complete it.

- **Bailout Strategy:** Trading your time for experience is just one way to move ahead in your career. If this approach doesn't fit your goals or style, consider one of the many other advancement approaches described in this book.

- **The "20 Percent Extra" Edge:** Decision makers are impressed by people with passion for their line of work. Saying, "I'd be willing to do this for free for a while," is a tough proposition to pass up. As a result, you have the power to create options where they didn't exist before.

- **"Go For It!" Bonus Activity:** Research several potential work-for-free options before presenting your proposal to increase your chances for landing the best work-for-free career advancement opportunity possible.

How to Trade Your Time for Career Advancement Opportunities

"If only I could have a chance to prove that I can succeed in the role I want." This is a popular wish among advancement-driven careerists. Ah, but finding an opportunity to prove yourself can be one of those chicken-and-egg challenges: You can't get hired until you have a demonstrated track record for success, yet you can't develop that success record until you've had a chance to try your hand in the new role. It's a frustrating dilemma!

One of the most effective solutions I've found to this quandary is to work for free—to take on the task you long to do, without expecting any compensation other than the chance to gain some valuable experience. This takes much of the pressure off of both you and the decision maker as you demonstrate your ability to succeed. Work-for-free opportunities can be structured as a-few-hours-per-week arrangements, or as more intense 20- to 40-hours-per-week commitments, depending on your interest and availability. The following sections offer how-to's for finding and landing a productive work-for-free opportunity.

Prepare and Present Your Work-for-Free Proposal

A step-by-step approach for creating and proposing a position is described in chapter 8. This same process—with a few small changes—will also work well for creating your work-for-free proposal. Review the proposal process described in chapter 8, and create lists of the following:

- **Experience you hope to gain:** This might include specific processes, skills, and knowledge you want to obtain.

- **What's in it for them:** Possibilities include an extra set of hands working toward the employer's business goals, additional help in areas where you already possess expertise, and a fresh perspective for solving problems or creating solutions.

Panic Point! Do you have a rough idea of the experience you want to gain, but don't feel as though you have enough details to put together a solid work-for-free proposal? If you're struggling to list the details, this might mean that you need to do a little more research to better define your career advancement goals. Reread chapter 3 to remind yourself of your career progress options and goals, and then consider researching specific learning opportunities by becoming active with professional associations (described in chapter 5), as well as by hav-ing information-gathering conversations with helpful networking contacts (see chapter 6 for more details). Once you've more clearly defined your CAP, outlining your objectives for a work-for-free proposal will be much easier.

Aim to split your proposed time and activities equally between gaining experience in your desired areas and providing the employer assistance in areas that will be beneficial to the organization. This will increase your chances for having your work-for-free proposal successfully received. Finally, in the moving-forward section, provide details about how your work-for-free offer would operate. Here's an example:

> In exchange for the opportunity to gain experience in these areas, I propose that I work for you, at no charge, for eight hours per week (one full day, preferably Wednesdays), over a period of two months. This would allow me to build my skills without putting any economic pressure on your organization. My aim would be to devote 50 percent of my time to gaining experience in the areas detailed in this proposal, and 50 percent of my time providing direct, useful support to your business.

To see a complete work-for-free proposal, check out the career champ profile later in this chapter, and be sure to review the "Practice and Present Your Proposal" section in chapter 8 for tips on having your offer received successfully.

Be Ready to Handle Questions and Objections

When you offer something for free, it can seem too good to be true, and some people will be wary of your intentions. They might bring up questions about your true motivations, as well as concerns about how they can protect their company information and processes. The following are some of the most popular objections and questions, as well as some possible responses:

Why would you want to work for free?

> One of my top priorities at this stage in my career is to learn how to _____. I see working for free as a win-win opportunity for the right company: I gain the experience I need while supporting your business with useful skills that will benefit you. Your business is my top choice for this opportunity, and I am hopeful that we can work out an arrangement.

Our liability insurance won't cover a non-employee working on-site.

Yes, I understand that is a limitation. I would be happy to sign an agreement releasing each other from any liabilities, if that would help.

> **Note:** Some businesses, especially larger organizations, won't be able to accommodate a work-for-free worker, due to insurance restrictions. Typically, smaller organizations, those with fewer than 25 employees, are your best bets for setting up work-for-free arrangements, because they have less red tape and boundaries. Another way to overcome this obstacle is to set up your work-for-free agreement through an educational institution, in the form of an internship. You might need to pay an internship class fee, yet many larger organizations already have procedures established for bringing on an intern, making it easier for you to have your proposal approved.

I don't want you stealing our formula for success.

This is a valid concern, and I would be happy to sign a noncompete contract that would prevent me from using your specific processes with another employer.

> **Note:** If you do end up signing some form of a noncompete agreement, consult with an attorney so that your agreement would be written to allow you enough flexibility to find employment in your desired area in the future, although not duplicating the exact processes you learned in your work-for-free arrangement.

I'm not so sure.

Fair enough. I know this is a big decision. Would you be willing to try it for a month or so, to see how it goes? We can agree to end it at any time if it's not working for one or both of us.

This just won't work for us.

That's okay. I truly appreciate you considering my request. Now that you know what I'm aiming to accomplish, would you be able to suggest any other people or companies I might talk with to set up something like this? I'm very motivated to make progress toward my career goals.

Why It's Worth Doing

"Work for free? No way! I deserve to be paid for my time and effort." I've heard this response from many clients when I propose that they take on a job or project strictly for its potential to help them move forward in their careers. And to some degree, they're right. Their time and effort *do* have value, and they should receive some compensation.

So how about if we look at this situation from a slightly different angle? Let's say that rather than receiving a paycheck, you instead earn compensation of a different sort: marketable experience—skills and know-how—that you'll actually be able to peddle for pay down the line. Would working for free make more sense to you if that was the case?

Also consider what you'd have to pay to take a class or to line up a formal internship through an educational institution in your desired career advancement arena. The experience you want to acquire might easily cost you thousands of dollars in tuition or course fees. Working for free allows you to gain that hands-on knowledge without paying a dime to a trade school or college.

Still not convinced? Okay then, let this percolate: When you work for free, you have the chance to not only build marketable, real-world skills but *also* demonstrate to decision makers that you can succeed with your new responsibilities. Once they've seen you in your new role, they'll be far more likely to offer you a job for pay later, as compared to hiring someone they haven't seen perform successfully. And in my experience, more than 50 percent of work-for-free arrangements turn into some form of paid opportunity. Those are pretty good odds, especially if your career advancement progress has stalled due to a lack of experience that you can gain by working for free.

Career Champ Profile: Nico

Nico, a chemist, was eager to gain experience in the use of a new diagnostic instrument that his company had just acquired. Knowing how to use this piece of equipment could open doors to better career opportunities for Nico, as the technology was gaining popularity in his industry. The challenge, though, was that Nico worked in a different department, and using the instrument wasn't part of his job responsibilities.

Determined to make progress toward his career advancement goals, Nico developed a list of the skills he wanted to learn, as well as a list of the experience he already possessed that could be useful to the other department. He then talked with his current boss about altering his start time each day, from 9:00 a.m. to 7:30 a.m. This would allow him to work an additional eight hours each week, from 3:30–5:30 p.m., Monday through Thursday, which he would do for no extra pay. Nico told his boss more about his desire to learn the new instrumentation, and his boss agreed to the shift change.

Nico then met with Teresa, the manager in the department where the new diagnostic system was located, and proposed his work-for-free idea. After talking through some logistical concerns, she agreed to try it for a month to see how it would work. Three months later, Nico had learned how to use the new equipment, and Teresa hired him full-time in her department. Five years later, Nico is still making successful progress in his career, related in large part to his knowledge of the diagnostic equipment he'd learned to operate by working for free. Figure 9.1 is the proposal Nico presented to Teresa.

Dr. Teresa Lamm
V.P. Drug Delivery
Ammond Labs
9945 Carepoint Way
Seattle, WA 98888

Dear Teresa,

As a satisfied employee of Ammond Labs, I am interested in maximizing my value to the organization, while maintaining my skills at a competitive level within the marketplace. To that end, I would like to propose that beginning in August, I devote eight hours each week (in addition to my regular work schedule) to learning how to successfully operate the new diagnostic equipment recently acquired by Ammond Labs. This would allow me to add to my expertise while providing the company with an additional employee capable of operating the equipment, if backup support is ever required.

Specifically, I would like to propose that Monday through Thursday I conduct my regular workday between 7:30 a.m. and 3:30 p.m., and then spend between 3:30 p.m. and 5:30 p.m. learning the new diagnostic equipment. I am willing to continue this arrangement for however long it takes me to become proficient in the operation of the equipment.

I would like to talk with you further about this possibility, and will follow up with you in the next few days to schedule a conversation. Thank you in advance for your consideration of my proposal.

Sincerely,

Nico Betts

Figure 9.1: Nico's proposal.

Core Courage Concept

Giving away your time and talents to gain experience takes guts. We naturally want to be compensated for the effort we put out. Yet sometimes, we need to make the first move to prove that we're truly worthy of achieving the goals we desire. By saying to a decision maker, "I am so committed to making progress in this area that I'm willing to do it for free," we prove to both ourselves and others, who can help us make the progress we want, that we're worth investing in.

Confidence Checklist

- ☐ Prepare and present your work-for-free proposal.
- ☐ Be ready to handle questions and objections.

Chapter 10

Launch Your Own Enterprise

Starting a business—small scale or larger—can be a useful strategy for achieving your career advancement goals. The creativity and responsibilities associated with business ownership allow you to craft your business to meet your talents and objectives. In this chapter, I'll introduce a few initial steps for defining and launching your own enterprise.

Risk It or Run From It?

- **Risk Rating:** If you keep your business tiny to begin with, the risk can be pretty low. If you attempt to take big leaps without having the experience and resources to back it up, the risk might be very high.

- **Payoff Potential:** Having your own business affords you many benefits that traditional employment doesn't: flexibility, creativity, and unlimited potential to grow professionally and financially.

- **Time to Complete:** You can complete the steps it takes to officially set up your business in just a few hours, but it can take years to establish your business as a successful entity.

- **Bailout Strategy:** Owning a business is optional. But before you ditch the idea as being too risky or overwhelming, at least

---

(continued)

(continued)

skim through this chapter to learn some business start-up basics, in case you ever change your mind.

- **The "20 Percent Extra" Edge:** Although it's a fact that most businesses will fail (more than 90 percent), the experience gained from defining and launching your own venture will be tools you can use throughout your career. Starting a business, even a tiny one, will help you stretch your skills to new levels.

- **"Go For It!" Bonus Activity:** Before jumping into your own enterprise, read books by business owners who have failed and succeeded to gain new insights and to increase your chances for success.

How to Get Your Business Started

The steps involved in starting a business can be pretty simple. It's the act of keeping it running successfully that is more difficult. The following sections offer suggestions for starting your enterprise on a strong foundation.

Evaluate the True Potential of Your Product or Service

I opened my first business when I was about 13 years old. I'd just learned how to make brightly colored, flour-clay sculptures. I thought they were so nifty, I figured everyone in the world would want one. Over a week's time, I produced an inventory of about 50 sculptures and then set up a stand to sell them on a busy street near my house. Within the first hour, two people stopped by to check out my wares. Both of them asked if the sculptures were meant to be eaten (they looked a lot like fancy sugar cookies). No one bought anything. After three hours, I loaded my wagon with my inventory and cardboard box stand, and trudged home, defeated. My clay sculpture business was a failure.

I started to learn an important lesson that day: Even though I thought a particular product would be appealing, that didn't mean anyone else would. Years later, when I opened my career counseling practice (and, by the way, I'd opened two other businesses before that, both of which also failed), I had a pretty good idea that there was a need for the services I'd be offering. I knew this because I'd been working as a career counselor for a company and had heard from several people that there were career services that individuals would be willing to pay for if only there was a business in the market to provide them.

So let's say, for instance, that you have what you believe is a good idea for a business. Before making any big decisions or taking any huge steps, answer the following questions:

- **What need or problem would I be addressing in the market?** My clay sculpture idea didn't address any need in the market, other than my desire to make them. On the other hand, when I considered starting a career counseling business, I'd been observing a need in the market for two years. Make sure that you can clearly articulate the need your business will address, and gather concrete evidence about the demand for it before diving in.

- **Who would I be selling to?** At 13, I had visions of mobs of people clambering to own one of my pieces of artwork, similar to the lines of customers lined up at my local Dairy Queen most summer evenings. But in reality, I'd never witnessed anyone *ever* showing an interest in buying a cute flour-clay sculpture — not once! When I started my career services business idea, I'd seen and heard, first hand, several people express interest in the kinds of services I would be offering. I could clearly define the age range, educational background, and needs of my target market. Who will your target market be, and how do you know they'll be interested in what you have to sell? Having solid answers to these questions can help you avoid business failure.

- **How would I make money?** At 13, my parents provided my flour and paints at no cost to me, plus every financial need in my life was being taken care of at that time. Without researching any market information on pricing for cute clay sculptures, I randomly picked a price of 50 cents per item, blissfully unaware of how this price would impact my business long term. If there was an actual demand for my sculptures, would I be able to cover my costs for materials, overhead, taxes, and labor year after year? Was 50 cents a price my target audience was willing to pay? I didn't know; I was clueless! Talking with thousands of people over the years, I've discovered that most don't even have a clear picture of the costs associated with running their own lives, let alone the financial pieces associated with running a successful business. Be sure you have a clear idea of your costs, as well as competitive market pricing, before proceeding.

- **How will you differentiate your business from what is already out there?** I had never seen a cardboard-box stand selling cute clay sculptures, so my young mind deduced that I had identified a brand-new market opportunity with huge amounts of potential. What I hadn't considered was *why* there were no other businesses like the one I was considering, and I discovered the answer to this question the hard way. Blazing a brand-new niche in the market can be expensive and risky. With my career services business idea, I knew what my competition had to offer. (I was employed by one of them!) And I could clearly see how I could offer new services that would set my business apart. In what ways will you be able to set yourself apart as a more desirable service or product provider?

- **What are my barriers to getting started?** At 13, I had the time, energy, and materials to launch my business, with no barriers (other than my naiveté) getting in my way. Yet in my 30s, as I considered what it would take to start a career counseling practice, there seemed to be too many barriers: I didn't know how to do bookkeeping; I was used to earning a certain amount of money each month, and that income supported my family; I didn't have any up-front capital to pay for office space, marketing activities, and a monthly stipend; and I knew I needed to complete certain government forms, but I was in the dark about which ones were relevant to my business and how to submit them. The barriers to your starting your business might seem overwhelming, but you can also view them as a checklist of things to troubleshoot to ultimately achieve your business-ownership goals.

- **Who would my competition be, and how much of a threat would they be?** As the owner of a clay sculpture business, I had lots of competition and didn't even realize it: lemonade-stand owners, who also had cardboard-box storefronts; bakeries and grocery stores, which sold items that looked like sugar cookies, yet could actually be eaten; novelty and drug stores selling nick-knacks and gift items; and craft stores, which sold materials and how-to books for other creative-types who wanted to make their own flour-clay sculptures. If I'd understood what I was up against at age 13, I probably would have stayed in my room happily playing with my Barbie dolls. Who will your competition be? The answer to this question can be tricky, because your competition isn't always obvious. For instance, my biggest competition in my career services business isn't another company, it's the do-it-yourselfers who believe they can achieve better results on their own, without paying someone for advice and help.

A trip to the reference desk at your local library or small business development center can help you understand who your competition might be, the potential of your idea, whether the market for your business is shrinking or growing, what format to choose for your business structure, and more, boosting your chances for ultimate business success.

Build Momentum Through Small Steps

If you were to look at a list of all of the steps necessary to launch and grow a successful business, you'd probably run away screaming. There are so many details to take care of, you could quickly become overwhelmed. Yet the saying "Eat an elephant one bite at a time" applies beautifully in business startups. The following steps can help you get your business rolling, without feeling as though it's going to bury you under too many activities:

- **Experience an exciting facet of your business ASAP.** Chances are, there's something about your business idea that's particularly intriguing to you: manufacturing a particular product, interfacing with customers to perform a service, or developing marketing materials that communicate your unique offering. Pinpoint an aspect of your potential business that seems especially inspiring, and then brainstorm ways that you can experience that activity as soon as possible: develop a prototype of your product, offer to perform a service for free, or mock up some marketing flyers. Jumping in on an exciting aspect of your business idea early on will allow you to verify that you'll truly enjoy the activity, because you might decide you don't like it once you actually do it. You'll also grow your expertise and build momentum to carry you through the other hoops you'll need to jump through to get your business started.

- **Tackle a business weakness.** After you've treated yourself to the exciting experience described in the preceding step, further increase your chances for long-term business success by shoring up a weak spot in your entrepreneurial background. You might hope that you'll be able to involve someone else to handle the tasks that you dislike, but early on, you'll probably need to wear all of the hats in your business: sales, marketing, administration, even cleaning the toilets. Does bookkeeping give you the willies, or does sales make you shudder? Tackle this weak spot before you officially begin your business by taking a skills-training class through a community college or the

Small Business Development Center. Or ask a successful business colleague to show you the ropes through some one-on-one training.

Complete the New-Biz Basics

Once you've experienced what you imagine to be a favorite aspect of your business idea (and you still like it), as well as lived through what you expect will be one of your toughest business tasks, you've passed two important hurdles toward long-term entrepreneurial success. Now it's time to put some business basics in place.

- **Choose a business name.** This can be one of the most exciting steps in starting a business. Yet you'll have to live with the name you choose for a long time, so choose wisely. The Internet can be a great resource for researching names that your competitors have chosen, as well as for helping you with ideas for your own business moniker. While you're at it, check out available Web addresses through a resource such as www.dotster. com to see which URLs may be available.

- **Choose and register your business structure.** Here's where things can start to get a little complicated, so you might want to seek professional guidance. You'll need to choose a business structure (sole proprietorship, limited liability company, partnership, and so on) that best supports the type of business you're considering. If you're a do-it-yourselfer, you can research the pros and cons of business formats to decide for yourself. If you want more direction, check with accounting and legal professionals for their recommendations. Once you've chosen your format, complete the federal, state, and city forms required to register your business legally. The Web site at www.business.gov is a great resource for the forms and information you'll need.

- **Obtain basic business tools.** A successful business owner once gave me a valuable piece of advice: If you don't take your business seriously, no one else will either. Looking back at my first three failed businesses (my dough-sculpture venture being the first), I realize now that I didn't treat them as if they stood a chance of succeeding. I didn't even have business cards to share with potential customers! If you truly want your business to stand a chance of making it, go to the trouble of setting up business basics. Order business cards (you can obtain inexpensive, professional cards at www.vistaprint.com), and set up a separate business bank account. Later you can add a Web site and dedicated phone line to your tools, but for now a bank account and business cards are the first essentials to put in place.

View Your Venture as an Adventure

In the beginning, your business will be fragile, like a newborn. Treat it carefully, and be patient as it develops. Despite all of the planning you might do in advance, you might need to drastically change your strategy to keep things rolling. Stay flexible and view the experience as an adventure, responding to day-to-day challenges as they present themselves. What can I do to keep moving forward while working toward achieving my career advancement goals? Your first business attempts might fail (the vast majority do), but don't let that stop you altogether. Catch your breath, learn from your experiences, and jump in again.

Why It's Worth Doing

In my opinion, everyone should have the experience of starting his or her own business, even if it's just a tiny enterprise dabbled in for an hour or two each week. Having a business allows you to develop professionally in ways being an employee can't. You experience taking ownership for an entity that is completely yours, being creative in solving your own problems and achieving your own goals, and benefiting (or suffering) from actions that were entirely decided by you. Even if your business fails, the majority of people who have started a business feel stronger about their career prospects and capabilities. It's well worth experiencing at least once in your lifetime.

Career Champ Profile: Shane

Shane had been employed as a social worker for almost a decade, yet for years he'd dreamed of having his own communications business, providing video, photography, and journalism services. We met to talk about how he could advance in this direction.

"Tell me who will buy your services and how you'll market to them," I asked early in our conversation. Shane pulled out a newspaper article featuring a local company owner who ran a similar-type business. "This guy says the market for his services is growing!" I asked if he had any other data to support future demand for the business Shane wanted to start. "Not yet," he replied.

Then I asked Shane what he knew about running a business. "Years ago I made and sold beadwork at local flea markets," he answered. So I asked, "Did you have a business license, separate bank accounts, a bookkeeping system, and a marketing strategy?" Shane laughed, "No, not really. I'd make about $100 a month—just fun money."

At that point in the conversation it was pretty clear that Shane had lots of work to do before quitting his day job and starting his communications business full time. We came up with a list of small steps he could begin to take: a trip to the business-information desk at his local library to research market information; sign up for a few community college classes in bookkeeping and marketing; start his business on a small scale, providing photography, video, and writing services to friends on the side. "This plan might take longer than I'd like it to," Shane told me as he gathered his notes, "but it feels more solid than what I had been working on; and ultimately, I want my business to be a success."

Core Courage Concept

Start a business...call it your own...be responsible for its success or failure...*yikes!* For a Career Coward, launching an enterprise can seem like an overwhelming step to take. Yet in the words of Mark Twain, "Do the thing you fear most, and the death of fear is certain." Start small, and even if your business crashes and burns, you can still say, "I was a business owner once." And great confidence comes from knowing that you at least gave it a good effort.

Confidence Checklist

☐ Evaluate the true potential of your product or service.

☐ Build momentum through small steps.

☐ View your venture as an adventure.

Part 3

Implement Your Plan and Reach Your Advancement Goals

Chapter 11

Implement and Refine Your CAP

Now that you've learned about the multitude of career advancement tools available to you, your head might be swimming with possibilities...but you feel as if you're drowning with all of the details. In this chapter, I'll walk you through a step-by-step list of the activities just described, so that you can decide which strategies are most relevant to you and what actions you want to take from here.

Risk It or Run From It?

- **Risk Rating:** This is a small-risk activity. You're still just planning, and you can always change your strategy if it ends up feeling too overwhelming to you.

- **Payoff Potential:** High—having a plan significantly increases your chances of overall success with your career advancement goals.

- **Time to Complete:** 20 to 30 minutes.

- **Bailout Strategy:** Using the techniques described in chapters 4 through 10, you can choose action items that will work for you and you can build your own CAP.

(continued)

(continued)

- **The "20 Percent Extra" Edge:** Analyzing the objectives in your initial CAP and linking them to specific activities and deadlines equip you with a solid, doable plan for achieving your career advancement goals.

- **"Go For It!" Bonus Activity:** Create an electronic file of your CAP, using word processing, spreadsheet, or project management software. Input all of your action items and deadlines, and keep this plan updated as you make progress on your CAP.

How to Improve the Strength of Your CAP

In the last several chapters, you've learned about several career advancement techniques and tools. Now you'll review and choose a number of them to use in achieving your career progress goals.

Select Strategies from Your Career Advancement Toolbox

The following is a summary list of the key techniques described in the previous chapters, presented in achievable action steps. Review the strategies described, check off those activities you've already completed, and identify which steps you want to build into the CAP you drafted in chapter 3. Also choose a target date for completion of each activity.

Analyze Your Past Career Successes and Frustrations

Activity	Target Completion
(from chapter 2)	
☐	Jot down a timeline of major activities that have occurred in your work and career, listing the main highlights.
☐	Use a 1–10 scale to rate the events on your timeline based on how energized or frustrated

Activity	Target Completion
	you felt at that time, with "1" being especially low and discouraged, and "10" being high energy and satisfied.
☐	Analyze why you were feeling the way you were feeling during the peaks and lows.

Itemize What You Value in Your Career

Activity	Target Completion
(from chapter 2)	
☐	Evaluate what you were focusing on, or neglecting, at the high and low times in your life.
☐	Determine holes in your career that you want to work on filling.
☐	Prioritize your top values.
☐	Write a few sentences about what each value means to you, to articulate your career advancement objectives.

Choose a Career Advancement Format

Activity	Target Completion
(from chapter 3)	
☐	Move up within your current career.
☐	Modify your existing work to make it a better fit for you.
☐	Expand into new territory within your existing work.
☐	Trade one career for two or more.
☐	Take a sabbatical to renew and gain a fresh perspective.
☐	Launch your own business.

(continued)

(continued)

Create a List of Career Needs and Put Together a Draft CAP

Activity   **Target Completion**

(from chapter 3)

- ☐   Refer to your prioritized values and their definitions and ask yourself, "What could I do to get closer to my ideal picture?" Create a long list of possible ideas.

- ☐   Repeat this process with your other values to create a draft list of action items.

- ☐   Draft your initial CAP, comprised of your overall career advancement goal and the ideas you brainstormed. Label the first part "Objective" and the second part "Action Plan."

Use Data Sources to Determine Individuals and Businesses You Need to Know

Activity   **Target Completion**

(from chapter 4)

- ☐   Yellow Pages listings, either online or hardcopy

- ☐   Local business directories, accessed online or through your area library resources

- ☐   Professional association membership directories

- ☐   Product or service catalogs

- ☐   Business databases such as Hoovers (www.hoovers.com) or Dow Jones (www.dowjonesfactiva.com)

- ☐   Your current employer's employee directory

Create a Target Database Including Key Information

Activity	**Target Completion**
(from chapter 4)	

- ☐ Organization/Contact Name
- ☐ Address
- ☐ Phone, e-mail, Web
- ☐ Summary of their purpose, mission, products, and services
- ☐ Key decision makers, particularly those related to your career advancement goals
- ☐ Additional relevant information

Consider Groups to Support Your Advancement Goals

Activity	**Target Completion**
(from chapter 5)	

- ☐ Civic organizations: Locally based groups focused on improving the community through a variety of volunteer and fund-raising activities (such as Rotary and Junior League).
- ☐ Business networking and Mastermind Groups: Might include chamber of commerce organizations and business networking groups, such as Business Networking International (BNI). Also consider finding or creating a mastermind group.
- ☐ Hobby clubs and nonprofit organizations: Choose groups based on your hobbies or beliefs.
- ☐ Professional associations: Consider international consortiums as well as small local groups based on either your specialty or industry.

(continued)

(continued)

Locate, Evaluate, and Join Groups

Activity	**Target Completion**
(from chapter 5)	
☐	Check out organizations' Web pages and surf for articles.
☐	Contact organizers or membership chairs to ask about their groups.
☐	Attend a meeting, just for fun.
☐	When you find a group that fits, participate actively in meetings, projects, and committees.
☐	Seek out people who can support your career goals, and set up one-on-one networking opportunities.

Begin You, Me, We Networking with Contacts

Activity	**Target Completion**
(from chapter 6)	
☐	Request networking conversations using a successful script: "I'm working toward achieving some career goals I've set for myself, and I'd like to talk with you to brainstorm some next steps. Would you be willing to meet me for coffee or talk with me on the phone sometime in the next few weeks?"
☐	Follow a proven networking agenda.
☐	You: Focus on the other person initially. Talk about FORD (Family, Occupation, Recreation, Dreams) topics.
☐	Me: Shift the focus back to you, as in, "Now I'm going to spend a few minutes talking about what's going on with me." Spend five minutes or less.

	We: You and your contact brainstorm together about next steps. Should take five minutes or less.

Analyze Educational Qualifications Needed

Activity	**Target Completion**
(from chapter 7)	
☐	Analyze job descriptions for the type(s) of position you'd ultimately like to land. Review popular job sites such as www.monster.com or www.jobfox.com. Create a listing of most-requested educational requirements.
☐	Conduct a quick survey with others already involved in those roles to find out what kind of training they've received.
☐	Determine what other skills or training you would need toward modifying your existing work to make it a better fit for you.

Investigate Several Avenues for Learning

Activity	**Target Completion**
(from chapter 7)	
☐	Formal degree and certificate programs
☐	Skill-building courses, offered through professional associations, community colleges, and organizations such as your local Small Business Development Center
☐	On-the-job training through the guidance of a mentor or coworker
☐	Self-instruction such as reading books on the subject or training yourself using instructional DVD or audio programs

(continued)

(continued)

Ask for Advice from Experts

Activity	Target Completion
(from chapter 7)	
☐	Run your plan by an expert or two who is experienced in your desired line of work before making any big decisions.

Define Your Position Proposal Objective

Activity	Target Completion
(from chapter 8)	
☐	Detail how you can be a resource to a company in a role that you propose. Decide the following:
☐	What activities do you want to be involved in?
☐	In what format do you want to execute these activities? (Full-time? Part-time? Partnership? Contractor?)
☐	How do you want to be compensated?

Determine "What's in It for Them"

Activity	Target Completion
(from chapter 9)	
☐	Show how your ideas can create a win-win opportunity for both sides. Brainstorm several potential benefits as part of your proposal development process based on these categories:

- Make money: How you might help them improve their revenues.

- Save money: How you could help them be more efficient to increase profitability and reduce waste.

- Improve quality: How your proposal would help boost their product or service quality.

- Improve image: How you could contribute to a better overall perception of their business.

Organize Your Position Proposal

Activity *(from chapter 8)*	**Target Completion**
☐	Compile your information in a professional, understandable proposal using a "You, Me, We" outline:
☐	You: In this section, include information that will be important to the recipient of your proposal, as in, "This is what's in it for YOU."
☐	Me: Here you'll outline what you hope to achieve through the proposal, as in, "This is what's in it for ME."
☐	We: Finally, you'll define what next steps you and your contact can take to move forward.

Practice and Present a Position Proposal

Activity *(from chapter 8)*	**Target Completion**
☐	Finalize your plan: Show your proposal to someone you trust and ask him or her for input on how to make it even better.
☐	Practice delivering your proposal: Pretend this is the real deal. Refine your proposal as necessary.
☐	Rehearse your closing: Practice wrapping up your proposal by saying, "What questions or concerns do you have? How can we move forward on this?"
☐	Anticipate objections, rejections, and questions: Be open to hearing, "I need time to think about it" and "I'm not sure this would work for us,"

(continued)

(continued)

Activity	Target Completion
	and be ready to ask further questions to learn more about the employer's needs and hopes.
☐	Schedule a conversation with the decision maker: "Boss, I have some ideas on how to increase our profitability. Could we meet for 30 minutes to go over my proposal?"
☐	Deliver it and move on: Chances are excellent that you'll make some progress toward your career advancement goals, one way or another.

Prepare and Present a Work-for-Free Proposal

Activity	Target Completion
(from chapter 9)	
☐	Gain hands-on experience through an unpaid internship or practicum experience by preparing a proposal that details the following:

- Activities in which you hope to gain experience. These might include specific processes, skills, and knowledge you want to obtain.

- What's in it for them: Possibilities include an extra set of hands working toward their business goals, additional help in areas where you already possess expertise, and a fresh perspective for solving problems or creating solutions.

Panic Point! Does it seem as if there are a crushing number of to-do items on your CAP action list? Do you feel discouraged at the amount of time and effort it will take to make real progress toward your goals? Keep in mind that you've just created what, for you, is most likely a *multiyear* CAP—you don't need to complete this in the next two weeks. View your plan as a long-term strategy for continuing to achieve motivating career successes, rather than as an overwhelming to-do list that you need to accomplish as soon as possible.

Finalize Your CAP

Now it's time to refine the draft plan you drafted in chapter 3 with the specific activities and deadlines you identified in the previous section to create a solid, effective CAP. In the next chapters, you'll begin to implement this plan and make exciting career progress.

Why It's Worth Doing

It's one thing to have hopes for how your career will progress…but it's quite another to have a plan, with specific activities and deadlines identified, to implement toward achieving it. The vast majority of people have hopes for how they want their careers to evolve, yet only a small percentage create and implement solid plans that will allow them to achieve those dreams. By analyzing and defining your career needs and opportunities, and compiling these into a workable strategy, you greatly increase your chances for actually achieving your career advancement goals.

Career Champ Profile: Maynard

In the early part of his career, Maynard worked as a civil engineer with a city government in the United States. But Maynard soon found himself itching to take on more complex projects, so he landed a position as a civil engineer for an international petroleum company overseeing mining projects in third-world countries. The challenges of the work were exciting to him, especially moving to a new part of the world every year or so and managing large-scale development projects. Yet after a few years of seeing the destruction of natural habitats his company was causing, as well as the poverty that many of the local residents lived in day to day, he chose to shift his construction management career in another direction.

At that point, Maynard set his career advancement goal to expand into a new territory in his existing work...but he wasn't yet sure what that new territory should be.

Over a period of several months, Maynard networked with colleagues in different industries, researching organizations and areas of expertise that seemed intriguing to him. In the process of this research, he came upon an intensive six-month MSBA—Master's in Sustainable Business Administration—program offered in the United States. This program would allow him to learn more about how to successfully run and manage businesses and programs that promoted and maintained practices that were sustainable for the planet.

Maynard presented this idea to his manager at the international petroleum company and requested a six-month sabbatical from his job to complete the program. His boss agreed, pointing out that the additional knowledge Maynard would gain might support valuable future growth within the company.

Core Courage Concept

Most people (me included) feel disheartened (and even a little angry) when they realize that it may take weeks, months, or even years of hard work to accomplish their career dreams. We live in an instant-gratification society, and we want results *now!* Yet here's another way to look at your situation: You can actually achieve results right *now*, simply by acting on one or more of the activities in your plan. While you might not achieve your long-term goal immediately, you will experience an immediate sense of satisfaction for the progress you made. And before you know it, your progress will be steady and rewarding...and your career advancement dreams will be coming true.

Confidence Checklist

☐ Select strategies from your career advancement toolbox.

☐ Finalize your CAP.

Chapter 12

Start to Make It Happen

Things are really beginning to come together. You've scoped out a customized, thorough CAP, and have learned about a wide range of tools to help you achieve it. Now you're at the starting gate, about to put your plan into action. In this chapter, I'll provide you with several proven, effective techniques for launching your plan successfully.

Risk It or Run From It?

- **Risk Rating:** Mid-range to low risk. You'll be taking baby steps, so you can decide how far you want to go at any one time.

- **Payoff Potential:** Fantastic! As my grandmother always said, "Begun is half done," and you're about to begin!

- **Time to Complete:** A few minutes to a few hours, depending on the tasks you tackle.

- **Bailout Strategy:** If for some reason you need to postpone beginning your plan, you can read through the end of this book and start your implementation later.

- **The "20 Percent Extra" Edge:** Having successful techniques for getting things started will improve your chances for satisfying progress.

(continued)

(continued)

> • **"Go For It!" Bonus Activity:** Think through other times in your life when you've made progress on career activities that were important to you. Analyze what kept you motivated during those projects, and then integrate the same strategies into your current CAP.

How to Launch Your CAP Successfully

Motivational speaker Sidney Madwed says, "We always do what we *most want* to do, whether or not we like what we are doing at each instant of our lives." Keeping this in mind, your challenge as you implement your CAP is to identify a step or two that you feel motivated to complete, and then build momentum from there. The following strategies will equip you with a range of techniques for choosing and moving ahead.

Prioritize and Itemize Your Career Action Plan Activities

As a first step to implementing your plan, review your CAP and the activities you've identified, and sort them based on the following:

• **Which activities need to happen first?** For instance, you won't be able to attend a professional association meeting until you first identify and research some possible groups.

• **Which activities will result in a higher payoff?** Setting up a cross-training session with a coworker might seem easier than researching, choosing, and beginning a degree program, but the degree will open more doors for you in the future.

• **Which activities are more urgent?** Although you might have both "Network with the VP at Jones, Inc." and "Write a position proposal for promotion within my company" activities on your list, creating the position proposal might be more urgent because you just heard that the company is planning an expansion, and it could be the perfect time for you to suggest a new position for yourself.

- **Which three to five activities make the most sense for you to start now?** Based on the analysis you've just completed — determining which tasks need to happen first, identifying which steps will result in a higher payoff, and prioritizing the activities that are more urgent — choose a few to work on first.

You can then improve your chances for beginning, completing, and succeeding with these action items using the following achievement-boosting techniques.

Capitalize on Your Strengths

What are you *really* great at doing? In which activities do you excel? What tasks do you willingly dive into because they're fun and rewarding for you? (If you're not sure of your answers to these questions, check out the strengths exercises suggested in chapter 2 to define a list for yourself.) If you know you're strong in a particular skill, you can use this asset to your advantage.

Let's say, for instance, that you're awesome at organization — you love to set up filing systems and data-tracking processes to maximize accuracy and efficiency. Knowing this, you could make your first activity in your CAP to design an entire information management system to support achievement of your goals. Or perhaps you're awesome at public speaking. Using this strength, you could work on developing and practicing scripts and meeting agendas to use when networking with helpful contacts.

Do the "Worst First"

Motivational speaker Brian Tracy is known for his "swallow two frogs every morning" approach to achieving your professional goals. His advice is to identify two to-do's each day that, although they might seem distasteful to you, will go a long way toward helping you make steady progress toward your objectives. He calls these unappetizing activities "frogs," and claims that if you swallow two early each day, they will fuel you through the rest of your day.

I've come to think of this strategy as "worst first," and when planning my day, I determine which tasks are important yet unappealing to me (often they're tasks that involve lots of detailed numbers — yuck!), and I tackle those first. And Brian Tracy is right; once I get those icky tasks over with, I feel more energized to take on the rest of my activities.

Reformat an Unpleasant Activity

I really don't like raw celery. When I see it on a plate of crudités, it gives me the willies! Yet there's one exception to my dislike of this vegetable: I love it chopped into tiny pieces and mixed into tuna salad.

In many cases, you can transform an intimidating or disagreeable task into something more palatable simply by changing how you approach it. As an example, while writing this book, I needed to conduct some research on a topic, and I dreaded doing it. This particular subject is one that for years I've steered clear of, primarily because the technique doesn't mesh well with my personal style. Still, others have had great success with it, so I knew it needed to be included in the book.

After procrastinating for months on doing the research, I reminded myself to take my own advice, and to challenge myself to come up with an approach that would seem more enjoyable. This led to the solution of rather than forcing myself to read several articles and books on the topic (a process that seemed especially unappealing to me), I could instead e-mail a few experts on the topic and ask for their insights. (I *love* asking experts for advice.) Within a few days, I had the information I needed, obtained through a method that was pleasing for me to execute.

Schedule a Standing Appointment with Yourself

A friend of mine is growing a business. Every Monday at noon she orders a lunch to be delivered, turns off her phone, and closes her office door. She then spends the next 90 minutes focusing solely on her business development to-do list, working diligently through the action items. Sometimes she uses this block of time to network with people important to her progress. Bottom line, she sets aside that time each week to focus on her career advancement priorities as a standing appointment with herself.

Consider creating your own weekly meeting with yourself. Setting aside that block of time will guarantee that you'll be able to make steady progress on achieving your CAP.

Delegate or Hire Help

The most successful people in the world don't do it all themselves. Rather, they delegate certain tasks to supporters able to get the job done, often better than they would have completed it themselves.

If the thought of setting up a networking meeting with a new contact freaks you out, for instance, then consider employing an appointment-setting service. One such company, Brickwork, allows you to hire assistants by the hour. I was once contacted by an assistant at Brickwork to schedule an appointment with a gentleman who wanted to network with me. Within minutes, the assistant and I had chosen a time, and the man who wanted to meet with me never had to go through the scary process of picking up the phone himself. He presented himself successfully during the networking meeting (it was the possibility of being rejected when requesting an appointment that had been a barrier for him), and overall, I was impressed with his creative approach to overcoming what could have been a show-stopping roadblock.

If certain activities seem overwhelming or distasteful to you, think about how you could delegate them to someone else: Hire a colleague to research a target list for you (you can connect with great resources through Craig's List); ask a friend to attend a professional association meeting with you, so that you don't have to go alone; contract with a professional writer to help you develop a powerful position proposal. If you feel stuck, collaborate with a helper.

Try the "Five-Minute Experiment"

Most people can endure practically anything for five minutes. Think about an activity that seems unpleasant to you. Then, when you find yourself facing that task, tell yourself that you'll only need to do it for five minutes, after which time you can decide if you want to continue.

For example, many people hate the idea of having to "work a room," meeting and making small talk with people at an event. Now imagine yourself walking into one of those gatherings, looking at your watch, and saying to yourself, "Okay, I'll do this for five minutes, and then I can quit if I choose to." Most people are willing to endure an activity for a few minutes. And often, once you've begun it, you decide to keep going.

Maximize Your Productivity

What factors help you to be most productive? Is it working at a specific time of day, or in a place where you're especially creative? Think through the criteria that help you perform at your best, and build in opportunities for you to succeed at your best potential.

For example, I'm a morning person. I'm most motivated and productive between 4 and 8 a.m. I also know that I feel most creative when I'm sitting in a cozy spot where I can have access to tea and snacks, such as in my writing corner at home or in a coffee shop. So when I have an important career advancement project to work on, I purposefully get up early and settle myself into my creative corner with my cup of tea. This setup gives me a jump-start on accomplishing the tasks on my list.

Break a Chore into Micro-Tasks

Some components of your CAP will seem insurmountable. Take creating a resource list of people and organizations, for instance. You might wonder, "How will I *ever* identify all of the people and businesses that can help me achieve my career goals? There are so many, there's no way I'll succeed with this!"

A task this large can seem impossible. Yet rather than aiming to succeed with the entire thing, strive to complete one teensy, weensy part of it—like finding and researching just five people or companies. Or if that seems too big, aspire to identify just one. And when you do, celebrate your micro-achievement (reward yourself with a latte, or a call to a good friend), and then take on the next micro-task.

Tell Others What You're Aiming to Do

Being accountable to others can serve as one of your strongest motivators. As you begin implementing your CAP activities, tell some of your best supporters—people you trust and who have your best interests in mind—about your career advancement goals and activities. Also ask them to check in with you occasionally about your progress, as in "How's the such and such project coming along?" Knowing that people you respect will be expecting to hear regular progress updates will help keep you on track and moving forward.

Reward Yourself for "Tough-Task" Successes

Some activities can seem especially challenging, such as calling someone important to request a networking meeting. To help you power through these tough chores, promise yourself a reward once you've completed it. Recently I had my own tough task to tackle; I needed to write a fairly long document describing a detailed process within my business. I put it off for more than two months, and finally made a deal with myself that once it was finished, I would reward myself with a shopping spree at my favorite consignment shop. It worked! Within two weeks, I'd knocked out the document, and was happily sporting my new-to-me attire.

Ask yourself, "What rewards would really help me get moving?" The answer might be a walk in the park, an e-mail to a good friend, or treating yourself to your favorite magazine. Then commit to giving yourself the payoff once you've conquered the challenging task.

Why It's Worth Doing

One way or another, you're going to have to invest some time and effort to achieve your career advancement objectives. Yet rather than working hard (and hating much of the process), it's to your advantage to find smarter, more motivating techniques for getting things done. In the long run, you'll have a much greater chance of succeeding with these approaches; plus, you'll have much more fun in the process.

Career Champ Profile: Deidre

Deidre, an attorney, had aspirations of advancing in her career by one day landing a position as a judge in the local court system. On a number of occasions, she saw postings for judge positions come open, but the application process was time consuming, and with her heavy workload, she couldn't seem to find the time to complete and submit the necessary applications.

Finally Deidre decided to delegate much of this task to someone else. She hired a qualified resume writer, spent an hour meeting with the specialist to go over what she wanted to communicate in her application materials, and then turned the writer loose to create a first draft of a curriculum vita, cover letter, and application. A few days later, the first draft was done, and Deidre needed to invest only another hour in reworking and finalizing the materials before submitting her application.

She was able to take important steps toward achieving her career advancement goals by hiring someone else to help, allowing Deidre to move past the time-crunch obstacle that had been holding her back.

Core Courage Concept

In many ways, coming up with a plan is the "easy" part of the career advancement. Putting goals and ideas on paper is a relatively low-risk process. Yet when it comes to actually beginning to work on your plan…well, that's where things can get a little tough. Knowing that you'll run into steps that seem overwhelming—and determining a strategy that will still allow you to keep moving forward—is what courage is all about.

Confidence Checklist

- ☐ Prioritize and itemize your career action plan activities.
- ☐ Capitalize on your strengths.
- ☐ Do the "worst first."
- ☐ Reformat an unpleasant activity.
- ☐ Schedule a standing appointment with yourself.
- ☐ Delegate or hire help.
- ☐ Try the "five-minute experiment."
- ☐ Maximize your productivity.
- ☐ Break a chore into micro-tasks.
- ☐ Tell others what you're aiming to do.
- ☐ Reward yourself for "tough-task" successes.

Chapter 13

Respond to Rejections, Obstacles, and Disappointments

T he farther you stretch yourself toward achieving your career goals, the more likely it is that you'll experience frustrations and disappointments. Then you have a choice: let your failures stop you in your tracks, leaving you with a lifelong feeling of bitterness, or find a way to work around the roadblock to achieve some measure of success. In this chapter, you'll learn several effective, inspiring strategies for picking up the pieces after a career catastrophe, to ultimately achieve the advancement successes you desire.

Risk It or Run From It?

- **Risk Rating:** Mid-range to high risk here. Responding poorly to disappointments can lead to stalled careers and lost opportunities.

- **Payoff Potential:** On the flip side, when you act purposefully after experiencing a career frustration, chances are very good that not only will you succeed, but your achievement will be even more satisfying.

(continued)

(continued)

- **Time to Complete:** A few hours to a number of months, depending on the strategy you implement.

- **Bailout Strategy:** Throw a pity party instead. It might feel good for a little while!

- **The "20 Percent Extra" Edge:** Rejection and disappointments are inevitable. Yet how you respond to them is completely up to you. See your disappointments as chances to learn, adapt, and persist (rather than as excuses for throwing in the towel), and impressive career successes will eventually come your way.

- **"Go For It!" Bonus Activity:** Dissect a number of your earlier career failures. What happened, and how did you respond? What were the ultimate outcomes? Chances are that you have a wealth of rebound strategies and success stories already in your career toolbox to draw upon and keep you moving forward.

How to Overcome Obstacles and Keep Progressing

As you move down the road of career advancement, there are many detours and barricades that can block your progress: The decision maker you present your proposal to says, "No." You decide after investing months into a career advancement project that it's not really what you want after all. You discover that the goal you set for yourself will take years, rather than weeks, to accomplish. Does it make sense to abandon your advancement efforts? Consider the following response strategies and then decide.

Respond Strategically When You Receive a Rejection

It takes a great deal of courage to put yourself out there by proposing yourself for a career opportunity. You might have invested hours of hard work in developing your plan, yet all it takes is just a few seconds for a decision maker to crush your dreams with a "no." When this happens, it can be tempting to want to figuratively (or literally) throw your proposal in the face of your rejecter and say, "I'm outta here!" Yet chances are you'd later regret burning that bridge. Instead, consider one of these responses:

- **Request the opportunity to revisit the idea at a later date.** When you receive a "no," ask "Would you be willing to talk about this idea again a few months from now?" Remember that you've been living with your innovative plan for a period of time, yet the decision maker might have just learned about it. Allow her a few months to digest what you've proposed, and you might eventually hear the "Let's go for it!" answer you were hoping for.

- **Present your plan to other potentially interested parties.** If the first decision maker you present your idea to declines, ask yourself, "Who else would be interested in this proposal?" Review the resource list you created in chapter 4 to identify other divisions, employers, or decision makers, and present your ideas to them.

- **Rework your plan to make it better.** When you receive a "no," ask, "What would make this proposal more appealing to you?" Be open to any ideas offered, and then decide if it makes sense to revise your ideas to incorporate their suggestions.

- **Consider "Plan B" (and "C" and "D").** Although your first proposal was rejected, another version of your plan might be just right for the decision maker's needs. Develop some alternative plans and then present those ideas for consideration.

- **Recall another time when you were rejected, as well as the ultimate result.** Like me, you can most likely remember a number of times when things didn't go as you'd initially planned — like the boyfriend who dumped me and the company who didn't offer me the job. But then recall what happened next, and ask yourself, "Did things turn out for the better after all?" Then think of times when the answer was "yes." The challenge is in having the patience to see what the better ending to your story will be.

Change Your Plan When You Discover It's Not What You Want After All

Let's say that you've spent time and effort diligently connecting with others in your industry, attending professional associations and networking with colleagues, in hopes of landing a next-rung-on-the-ladder position within your specialty. Yet the more time you've put into this career advancement project, the more you hear your inner voice saying, "This just doesn't feel right!"

Changing your mind after launching into a CAP is more common than you might think. It's perfectly acceptable (and better for you in the long run) to listen to your instincts about what's right for you, rather than heading down the wrong path. If you discover your original plan is the wrong fit, use the information you've acquired to revise your plan and goals.

As a first step toward correcting your course, review and rework the steps outlined in chapters 1 through 3 to develop an improved plan. Let's say, for instance, that rather than landing a position with more pay and responsibility, you've changed your mind and now want to start your own business, working as a consultant. Your new career advancement format goal now is becoming an entrepreneur.

In this example, you next review your values and determine that Balance—having more control over your schedule and activities—is a higher priority for you than Belonging—being a part of a group. These new insights, which have become clearer to you as a result of having implemented your first CAP, can now be integrated into a new and improved plan. And rather than viewing your first attempt as a failed effort, realize that you're on your way to achieving an overall better result.

Bounce Back After Being Passed Over for a Promotion

A friend of mine uses the acronym POPO (Passed Over, Pissed Off) for someone who gets skipped over for a much-deserved promotion and is extremely ticked off as a result. Not being chosen for an opportunity you felt was a shoe-in for you can leave you feeling resentful toward the world. While you have every right to feel angry at being rejected, carrying around a chip on your shoulder has the potential to destroy your chances for future opportunities.

It's easy to say, "Ah, I'll just get over it," yet in reality a significant disappointment can turn out to be an emotional weight that you drag around for years. The following strategies can help you truly push through and overcome a POPO frustration:

- **Vent your disappointment in a productive way.** Complaining to coworkers about getting passed over could come back to haunt you. Instead, talk with a friend who you can trust to keep your comments confidential, preferably someone who's not involved in your career field or company at all. Talking with a counselor, or journaling about your disappointment, are other productive methods for processing your dissatisfaction. Whatever method you choose, find some way to articulate and sort out your aggravations.

- **Rather than getting angry, get busy.** There was some reason why you weren't chosen for the opportunity. Maybe you lack a particular skill or degree, you interviewed poorly, or you're not buddies with the hiring manager. Whatever the reason (and chances are you have a pretty good idea of what this is), there's some positive action you can take in response. Get more training, improve your interviewing techniques, or work toward moving into another organization that values performance over favoritism.

- **Move on.** If you had your heart set on a goal that your current employer isn't supporting, it might make sense to switch companies to achieve your objective. *The Career Coward's Guide to*

Resumes, The Career Coward's Guide to Interviewing, and *The Career Coward's Guide to Job Searching* provide outstanding strategies and guidance for targeting, presenting yourself for, and landing a position that would allow you to realize your goals.

Maintain Momentum Even When It's Taking a Long Time to Achieve Your Goals

When I first opened my career counseling practice, I had visions of creating a thriving, profitable business within a year. I pictured myself meeting numerous clients each day, with phones ringing off the hook as new clients called to schedule appointments with me. I also imagined presenting workshops to hundreds of people who were hungry to hear about the wisdom I had to offer regarding their careers. "By this time next year," I thought to myself, "my business will be a *huge* success!"

Yet 12 months passed and my business was doing okay, but it wasn't booming. In fact, I was struggling to simply learn how to use my bookkeeping software. And when I scheduled a workshop, I was thrilled when 10 people showed. While I could say that my business had grown in the last year, it certainly wasn't the raging success I'd imagined.

Ten years later (yes, 10 years), my business is now beginning to look like the vision I'd imagined originally. Saying that things have taken longer then I expected is an understatement. Still, I wouldn't trade the experience for anything, and looking back, I can have these insights about things taking longer than expected:

- **Track the progress you have made.** If you're attempting a career progress goal you've never attempted before, you really have no idea how long it will take. You might set a hoped-for deadline for yourself, but it's really just a guess. Readjust your timeline when you have more data about how events are progressing.

- **Seek out information on how to speed things up.** If you're frustrated at the pace of your progress, look for information, resources, and people who might be able to help you boost your rate of accomplishment. Ask others, "Do you have any ideas for how I can make this happen faster?" and research examples of other people who have attained speedy success.

- **Enjoy the journey for what it is.** Looking back over my own 10-year business-growth adventure, I can see now that there were many skills that I needed to master before I could move on to the next challenge. While my business growth might not have happened as fast as I thought it would, I wouldn't trade those learning experiences for anything. Like me, you might discover that the process of getting to where you want to go can end up being the true accomplishment.

Why It's Worth Doing

Whenever I run into a roadblock on a plan or proposal I've presented, my initial reaction is frustration. "Argghhh!" I think to myself. "Why didn't this fly?" Then, usually within a few minutes, a light bulb goes off in my head—almost literally, a light bulb—and I remind myself of how many times Thomas Edison tried to make a light bulb that would work. Did he put together one plan, have it fail, and then give up? Or did he make two attempts, and then ditch his idea? No, Edison made more than 1,000 tries before his light bulb idea succeeded.

If you're truly, passionately devoted to your career advancement goal, then one failure (or two, or several) won't be enough to stop you. Like Edison, you'll study your strategy, make adjustments, and then try, try again. Because when you achieve the career goal you've set for yourself, you—and the world—will be brighter.

Career Champ Profile: Seth

Seth devoted two years to completing his master's degree in conflict resolution, with the career advancement goal of landing a job as a mediation specialist within a city government organization. Yet a year after graduation, Seth was still actively job searching and had made very little progress. "I've discovered this position is just so specialized," he told me. "Only a few positions open up each year across the country, and hundreds of candidates are applying for them. It could be years before I land a job in this field."

Seth was pretty frustrated, and he spent a week venting about his situation with a few close friends. Then, rather than staying angry and stuck, Seth decided to get busy. He spent an afternoon on the Internet, researching the backgrounds and credentials of people working in the field of mediation and conflict resolution, and he also investigated how they were applying their skills and knowledge. Through this exercise, he discovered that several of the specialists had training in neurolinguistic programming (NLP), a technique that allowed them to support their clients not only through the conflict resolution process, but also with gaining new skills for reframing negative situations and taking steps to grow personally.

Seth loved the idea of being able to offer this kind of support to his mediation clients. In the next few months, he located and completed two NLP training courses. In the second class, he met a gentleman who worked for a consulting firm that provided mediation training and employee relations support services for businesses. Seth's new contact told him the company was expanding and that he might be a great fit for a position with the company.

A month later, Seth accepted a job with the consulting firm, in a position that was much more exciting and rewarding than the government position he'd been aiming for originally. His Plan B—which he'd never considered before experiencing a career disappointment—turned out to be a much better fit for his overall professional goals.

Core Courage Concept

It takes less time, energy, and courage to abandon your CAP when you encounter a roadblock than it takes to retreat, regroup, and try again. But the easy way out is rarely the most rewarding. When disappointment strikes, allow yourself some time to feel frustrated, but then gear yourself up to attempt your goal again. It's likely that the satisfaction you'll ultimately feel for achieving your goals will far exceed the effort it took to attain them.

Confidence Checklist

☐ Respond strategically when you receive a rejection.

☐ Change your plan when you discover it's not what you want after all.

☐ Maintain momentum even when it's taking a long time to achieve your goals.

Chapter 14

Take Advantage of Unforeseen Career Growth Opportunities

You've got your solid, motivating CAP in place, and you've been making steady progress toward your goals. Then, out of nowhere, an opportunity pops up that you had never considered before: a chance to perform a completely different position in a totally different industry...the possibility of relocating to a different continent to support an important cause...or the option to buy into a business opportunity in an entirely new industry. Whatever the possibility, it's miles outside of the scope of your original plan, and you're in a panic over what to do. This chapter will show you how to sort through and respond successfully to unplanned-for possibilities.

Risk It or Run From It?

- **Risk Rating:** Changing course to capitalize on a new plan can be extremely risky; yet it can also offer paybacks you never could have dreamed of before.

(continued)

(continued)

- **Payoff Potential:** The outcome could be better or worse than you expected, so be sure to stick to your values as you make important career decisions.

- **Time to Complete:** The timelines will vary depending on the activities you choose to pursue.

- **Bailout Strategy:** Stick closely to your CAP—although you might end up missing out on some pretty exciting opportunities if you don't at least consider unexpected possibilities.

- **The "20 Percent Extra" Edge:** Saying "no" to opportunities that fall outside of your original CAP is easy—but not necessarily the best strategy. Taking the time to gather more information and consider opportunities could lead you down an even better path than you'd considered before.

- **"Go For It!" Bonus Activity:** Interview a few people you admire, and ask them about the unforeseen opportunities that have popped up in their careers, and learn how they decided whether to act on them or let them pass.

How to Evaluate and Respond to Unplanned-for Possibilities

Opportunities present themselves every day, but it's up to us to recognize and respond to them. Like trying on exciting new fashions you'd never considered before, the following steps can help you look at your career possibilities in different—and possibly more attractive—ways.

Evaluate the Opportunity Against Your Vision and Values

When out-of-the-box career options present themselves, it's helpful to filter possibilities through your personal vision-and-values criteria. To accomplish this, review your list of values from chapter 2, as well as your career vision statement from chapter 3, evaluating this new opportunity against your overall CAP. For example, let's say that you've defined the following vision and values for your career:

> It is my career advancement goal to progress within the field of manufacturing engineering, achieving numerous professional accomplishments which gain me the respect of my colleagues and leadership. As part of this progress, I aim to continue to improve my value to my employer organization so that I can achieve and earn greater financial worth.

...and you've listed your top values as these:

> Security, knowledge, creativity, success, and growth.

To this point, it's been your plan to work diligently to earn promotions and land positions at employer companies who can offer you increasing levels of challenge and pay. Then one day you receive the following e-mail from Nolan, a former coworker:

> I'm launching an exciting company that will manufacture a line of engine-performance products for the boating industry. I think you'd be an excellent member of my team of founders, serving as director of manufacturing. I'd need you to make an initial investment of $25,000 to help fund the business, and you wouldn't be able to take home any money in the first two years, but I foresee plenty of financial rewards after that. In fact, I project sales of $2 million within five years, with annual salaries for the founders of $250K plus bonuses. Interested?

For someone who's been focused on climbing the corporate ladder, this opportunity might seem both exciting and overwhelming: A $25K investment! No earnings for the first 24 months? But you'd also have the chance to be taking home a quarter of a million dollars within five years. What to do, what to do?

This is a crucial time in your decision-making process. Given the newness and unfamiliarity of this idea, your first inclination might be to reject it, just so you won't have to deal with the pressure of choosing. Yet you might stand to miss out on the opportunity of a lifetime.

For this reason, it's essential to think things through as level-headedly as possible.

Reread your vision, asking yourself, "Is this opportunity at all on track for what I want to create in my career?" On paper, this opportunity seems to line up nicely with the stated career advancement vision, so the possibility has successfully passed through the first decision filter.

Next, put the opportunity to the values test, evaluating it against your top priorities: security, knowledge, creativity, success, and growth. Clearly, you would be making good use of your knowledge and creativity in a position like this. And if the company thrived, you would achieve your success and growth goals.

But what about security? In particular, you're being asked to put up $25K of your hard-earned money, with no guarantee of any return at all, not to mention having no income for two years. This part of the deal feels highly risky to you. Will the lack of security be a deal-killer? It might be. To flesh the opportunity out further, you'll want to gather more information before you can decide.

Make a List of Your Questions and Concerns

Often, when I'm struggling to make a decision, my engineer husband will say, "You don't have enough data to make a decision." This is typically the case for most of us. When we don't have enough information, it's nearly impossible to make a good choice. As you consider an unplanned-for career possibility, give yourself the chance to learn as much as you can about the opportunity before forcing yourself to choose.

Consider the preceding business buy-in example, for instance. What else would you want to know before you would be able to make a decision? Here's a list of sample questions:

- Do I have enough money for the initial investment, as well as to carry myself through for two years? If not, how could I get it if I wanted to?

- What is Nolan's track record in ventures like this? What are the backgrounds of the other investors?

- What products are they considering producing, and what's the potential in the market for them?

- What exactly would my role in the company be?

- What if I bought in and then decided that I wanted to step out? What would the process for that be?

Having answers to these questions would definitely help with my ability to decide Yea or Nay to the business opportunity.

Panic Point! Do you worry that you'd *never* have enough data to make a confident decision on an important career decision, because there are just too many unknowns? With all of the factors that can come into play with a significant career choice, gathering enough information can feel like an impossible task. Yet keep in mind that by simply going through the process of itemizing questions and collecting data, you greatly improve your chances for securing that key piece of information that will help you make a decision that's right for you. Although you may never be able to gather *all* of the information you'd like to have, you do stand a very good chance of collecting enough to move forward.

Create an Objective Analysis of the Risks and Opportunities

After you've made a reasonable effort to obtain answers to your questions and concerns, it's time to summarize your information and move toward a decision. The old-school Pros and Cons list still serves as one of the best analysis tools. Focus on the plusses and minuses related to your values:

Pros of Opportunity

- I'd get to apply more of my creativity toward solving man- ufacturing challenges than I get to now.

- I have enough money to fund my buy-in investment, and to live on for two years, thanks to prioritizing savings and living frugally.

- This will be the second start- up venture for Nolan, and his first one was a huge success (he recently sold the company for a nice profit).

- Ultimately, this venture could turn out to be a huge success, putting me way ahead of where I am now career-wise.

Cons of Opportunity

- For a while, I'd have to work with used or dated manufac- turing technology, as we conserve funds during our start-up phase.

- I stand to lose a large chunk of the financial security I've built up for myself over the last 10 years.

- My career growth will be limit- ed for a while. I may not be able to participate in profes- sional conferences and training courses, putting me behind my peers on the latest advances in manufacturing. This would be a problem if I ended up seeking employment again at some time.

Because it's difficult to maintain an objective perspective while you're in the thick of making an important career decision, it's wise to seek the guidance of others you trust: your accountant, lawyer, mentor, or a respected business colleague. Present your pro and con data and ask for their opinions, as well as their input on key factors you may not have considered. Ideally it's best to get feedback from at least three people and to spend a period of time contemplating their input before you move forward.

Be Aware of Your Bailout Strategies

Years ago, when I was thinking about leaving my paid job as a career counselor to open my own practice, I spent months agonizing over what might happen: specifically, that my business would flop and that I'd have no income—plus a damaged ego to deal with. "Woe is me...what will I do?" I fretted, day after day.

Then one morning I awoke with a new insight that simplified my decision-making challenge: If my business failed, I could always go back to working as an employee, either with my former career counseling firm or in my previous marketing career, or even at a fast-food restaurant. There was no law that said once I made a decision to open a career counseling business, I had to live with my choice forever. I could always backtrack to one of my former positions if I chose to. Once I looked at the opportunity from that perspective, it was easy to make the decision to move forward on starting my own practice.

As part of your decision-making process, keep in mind that if the new opportunity doesn't work out, returning to your former career plan is almost always an option.

Why It's Worth Doing

For more than a decade, Regan, one of my colleagues, ran a successful human resources consulting company. Her business was well respected, provided her a good income, and seemed to be highly satisfying to her. I figured Regan would continue to grow her business over the years, achieving greater and greater levels of reward, and eventually retire knowing that she'd created something successful and impressive. Yet over lunch one day, a mutual friend informed me that Regan was selling her consulting company and had accepted a position as CEO of a newly founded medical instrumentation business. Over the next year, we watched with admiration as Regan nurtured the fledgling enterprise along. Then, just when we'd gotten used to the idea of Regan as a start-up CEO, she switched gears again, handing over her leadership role to another manager in the company and signing up for an intensive language-training program that would prepare her to teach English to children in third-world countries.

Eventually I crossed paths with the very busy Regan and asked her about her evolving (and exciting) career path. "These opportunities have all just seemed like a good use of my talents, plus they meet my life goals—helping people develop themselves as I develop myself in the process." Regan was clearly progressing in her career, although not along a traditional climb-the-corporate-ladder route. Instead, she seemed to be advancing through fun excursions in hot-air balloons, kayaks, and rickshaws!

I've learned so much from Regan about career progress—primarily, that implementing my original CAP isn't the primary goal. Rather it's honoring my priorities and life mission, and being open to a variety of opportunities that fit those criteria, even though they may look different than what I'd originally planned for myself.

Career Champ Profile: Sybil

Sybil had created a successful career for herself as a manager of a medical practice, overseeing groups of physicians and their clinics and providing quality medical care for a healthy profit. Her CAP called for landing management positions with even larger medical organizations, taking on greater and greater responsibilities, and earning higher pay. Then one day Sybil was approached by a company that was in the process of launching home-care franchises nationwide, asking if she'd be interested in buying the rights in her city.

At first the idea seemed absurd to Sybil; she was used to receiving steady, sizable paychecks for the management expertise she provided and having large, capable teams of experts to assist her in achieving the organizational goals set for her. Opening a tiny home-care business, staffed with just herself and one support person, seemed ridiculous and completely outside of what Sybil had been planning for herself.

But instead of saying "No way!" immediately, Sybil told the franchise business owners that she'd think about it. Then she reviewed her career vision—to use her medical and management expertise to provide quality, profitable health care—and determined that owning a home-care agency fell within that scope. Then she spent a few afternoons researching the home-care industry and local providers, gathering information off the Internet and through reference documents at her local library. The more data she gathered, the more excited she became about the opportunity.

Sybil then evaluated the facts she'd gathered against her top values: health, professionalism, happiness, financial independence, and helpfulness. She was especially excited about the potential to be even happier in her work, at the prospect of not having to deal with demanding physicians day to day. Everything else seemed to line up well also, except for financial independence; the idea of owning a small business, and the potential for financial failure, seemed like a deal killer to Sybil. She talked about this concern with the franchise business owners. In response, they showed her data that demonstrated that of the 50+ home-care franchisees in operation over the last five years, more than 90 percent of them were currently profitable and successful. The proven business model they would provide to Sybil as part of her franchise ownership would significantly reduce her risk of financial failure.

Three years later, Sybil is happily and successfully running her own home-care business—a career opportunity she hadn't imagined for herself initially, but one that fit her career advancement goals after she'd considered it more carefully.

Core Courage Concept

It takes guts to seriously consider unplanned-for career possibilities without immediately dismissing them as unworkable or too risky. It can seem so much easier to stay on a calculated path, figuring that it's better to be safe than sorry. Yet life—especially when you're actively involved in advancing yourself—can hand you promising, surprising possibilities. Knowing how to evaluate and process them based on your vision and values will lead to even more rewarding career successes than you'd ever imagined before.

Confidence Checklist

☐ Evaluate the opportunity against your vision and values.

☐ Create an objective analysis of the risks and opportunities.

☐ Be aware of your bailout strategies.

Chapter 15

Succeed and Repeat!

If you've implemented just a few of the steps described throughout this book, chances are you're already beginning to achieve some important career advancement successes. Congratulations! Keep this momentum going, and achieve greater and greater career successes, through the simple activities outlined in this chapter.

Risk It or Run From It?

- **Risk Rating:** Low to mid-range risk, depending on the activities you choose.

- **Payoff Potential:** A lifetime of rewarding, motivating career progress.

- **Time to Complete:** Years and years (this is an ongoing process).

- **Bailout Strategy:** Stay in your current situation without purposefully steering it. Hope that interesting opportunities come your way. Live your career by chance rather than by choice.

- **The "20 Percent Extra" Edge:** By putting just a small amount of time and attention into your CAP month after

---

(continued)

(continued)

> month, and year after year, the small steps you take can add up
> to huge progress.
>
> - **"Go For It!" Bonus Activity:** Begin writing an autobiogra-
>   phy of your career and life adventures. Add in your career
>   successes as they evolve, and you'll be able to track the
>   impressive life you're creating for yourself.

How to Keep Your Career "Green and Growing"

There's the saying, "If you're not green and growing, you're ripe and rotten." Chances are, you'll be involved in your career for decades, working year after year to accomplish the goals your employers and customers set for you. You can, like most workers, drift down the river of your career experiences, waiting to see what comes along and how you'll respond. Or, with just a bit more planning and effort, you can create and achieve career accomplishments that are hugely satisfying. Here are a few strategies to help you stay on course and attain your career dreams.

Review and Revise Your Career Advancement Plan

You've already invested a good deal of effort into developing and acting on your CAP. As you've implemented steps in your plan, you've created some valuable momentum in your career. Don't let this precious forward progress go to waste! At least once each month, review your CAP to evaluate whether your strategy is still on target for what you truly want to accomplish. This is also an excellent opportunity to determine which action items to focus on at that time.

There's a strong possibility that, over time, your interest in achieving certain aspects of your CAP will shift. A priority that seemed important to you one year may lose its appeal the next. This can be especially true when you experience big changes in your life: getting married or divorced, having children or experiencing a health issue, or discovering a new personal or professional interest that leads to a desire to involve yourself in new arenas. When you discover that your old CAP seems off base for your present life experiences, redo the priority-setting activities in chapter 2 and the development exercises in chapter 3 to create a new-and-improved CAP that is appropriate for your life at that time.

Make Steady Progress on Your CAP Action Items

At any given moment, you'll have several action items to complete in your CAP. Yet it's impossible (and inefficient) to take steps on all of them at once. How will you decide which ones deserve your attention first, second, and so on? The following system will help you prioritize and progress through the most important components of your advancement plan:

1. **Review your career advancement goals.** In chapter 3 you created your CAP, including several important action items related to your progress. Look over what you defined at that time as a reminder of what you're aiming for.

2. **Write out a complete list of all the action items currently included in your CAP.** For instance, from the sample CAP included in chapter 3, this would be my list:

   - Continue to participate in the monthly mentoring group of which I'm a member.

   - Research a few professional associations that would be made up of business owners in a similar industry to mine: career services. Maybe join and become an active member.

   - Take a course, or read some books, on effective ways to publicize my books.

- Research some authors whose books have done extremely well and find out how they grew the success of their books.

- Work with my publicists more actively to identify ways that I can improve the sales results of my books.

- Create some goals for what I want my financial picture to look like.

- Take a few classes, or read a few books, to learn more about what I need to know.

- Schedule a few hours each month to review my financial status against my goals and determine any action items I need to take in the next month.

- Continue writing and creating career materials: books, articles, and tools.

- Complete my Licensed Professional Counselor credential.

- Investigate the logistics and worth of getting a Ph.D. in a related field.

- Maintain a successful balance of work and home activities, regularly reevaluating the needs of each by conferring with the key people in my life.

- Set up quality-checking systems to ensure that the work my business performs for clients maintains my desired levels of integrity.

3. **Determine the significance of each item on your list.** Each opportunity has a different level of "value" to you, depending on its potential to help you achieve your career advancement goals. You can evaluate opportunities based on two criteria, importance and urgency, to help you decide how to prioritize your activities. For instance, you can rank the importance of an opportunity based on how closely it matches your career advancement goals, using an A, B, and C rating. And in terms of urgency, you can use a 1, 2, 3 ranking system, with 1 being

extremely urgent, 2 being less urgent, and so on. To help you decide how to rank the action items, evaluate each item against your list of prioritized values, which you created in chapter 2. Using this ranking system, I rated the items on my list in this way:

- Maintain a successful balance of work and home activities, regularly reevaluating the needs of each by conferring with the key people in my life. *A1*

- Work with my publicists more actively to identify ways that I can improve the sales results of my books. *A1*

- Create some goals for what I want my financial picture to look like. *A2*

- Take a few classes, or read a few books, to learn more about what I need to know. *A2*

- Continue to participate in the monthly mentoring group of which I'm a member. *A2*

- Take a course, or read some books, on effective ways to publicize my books. *A2*

- Research some authors whose books have done extremely well and find out how they grew the success of their books. *A2*

- Schedule a few hours each month to review my financial status against my goals and determine any action items I need to take in the next month. *A2*

- Set up quality-checking systems to ensure that the work my business performs for clients maintains my desired levels of integrity. *A2*

- Continue writing and creating career materials: books, articles, tools. *A2*

- Research a few professional associations that would be made up of business owners in a similar industry to mine:

career services. Maybe join and become an active member. *B2*

- Complete my Licensed Professional Counselor credential. *B3*

- Investigate the logistics and worth of getting a Ph.D. in a related field. *B3*

Once you have your action list prioritized, you'll have a clear plan for where to invest your time first, next, and so on. Using this system can make career-activity action planning easy.

Develop and Maintain a Success Database

As you experience more and more in your career, recording your accomplishments can be a wise investment of your time. Not only does it feel great to have evidence of your successes (which is especially nice to review when you're feeling frustrated or low), this record of your triumphs can also come in handy as you work toward achieving future career advancement goals.

A success database is a collection of your achievements, recorded in an electronic database, hardcopy portfolio, or even a scrapbook. For additional ideas on how to create and maintain a success database, check out the suggestions included in *The Career Coward's Guide to Interviewing*.

Another advantage to creating and maintaining a success database is that it allows you to recognize and celebrate your successes. When you've made progress in your career—on a small, mid-level, or larger scale—celebrate it! We could all use a few more celebrations in our lives.

Take Occasional Trips Outside Your Comfort Zone

Although it's important to stay focused on your CAP, it can be just as valuable to open yourself up to new possibilities and experiences. Take a sincere interest in meeting people from a variety of specialties

and walks of life. Learn about what's been important and meaningful to them. When you discover new, intriguing arenas, give yourself
the opportunity to gather additional information by researching and
reading a few articles, attending a meeting or visiting a facility,
signing up for a small-scale volunteer project, or interviewing a specialist. Regularly exposing yourself to new areas can open new doors
of interest and possibilities, as well as help you confirm that you're
on the right career advancement track for you.

Panic Point! You may still be wrestling with the question, "Are my career advancement goals truly the *best*
plan for me?" Because there are so many options available to you, it's natural to wonder whether the choices
you're making are the *best* ones. Yet keep in mind that
there are literally millions of career plans and choices you
could choose for yourself, and that there's no single
"right" formula for career success. As long as your CAP
and its related activities are in line with your highest values—and you're honoring what's most meaningful and
important to you—you'll truly be succeeding with your
career advancement goals.

Why It's Worth Doing

A few years ago, I reviewed my career advancement plan with my
husband. We both agreed that my career-counseling office location
at that time was less than ideal: I was operating out of a one-room
sublet location with zero street signage, and my part-time contract
worker and myself were bursting at the seams. I also disliked paying
rent on the space every month and was motivated to find something
that we could purchase instead. We agreed that one of my career
advancement goals for the year would be to locate and buy a new
office location. We even had a vision in mind for what we wanted to
find: There was a smallish green house in my town that had been
built in the early 1900s and had been converted to a professional
office space. It was just the right size, and was located on a street

that experienced a high level of drive-by traffic. We both agreed we'd love to find something just like it.

Over the next few months, I looked at a variety of properties. I compared everything to the little green office house, with the aim of finding something similar. "How does the location stack up...the size...the ambiance?" I came close to finding the right kind of property a few times, but then some snafu would pop up to ruin the deal. Still, I kept on looking.

One day about three months later, I saw a "for sale" sign in front of the little green office house. Within 24 hours, my husband and I had looked at it and made an offer, and two months later, I moved my office to our new location.

An inspiring, well-developed CAP does you little good if it's being ignored on a shelf somewhere. Reviewing it regularly, and refining it as necessary, takes just a little time and effort throughout the year. Yet the payoffs can be *enormous*, as I experienced by keeping my eye on a career advancement goal for my business. By routinely reminding yourself of what you want to achieve in your career, and prioritizing where you need to invest your energy, you can recognize and respond to the right kind of opportunities as they present themselves.

Career Champ Profile: Luisa

Luisa's career had evolved over a number of decades. After completing her undergraduate degree, she took a position with her local university working as a staff member with one of the school's student support programs. She enjoyed her career well enough to work steadily toward completing a master's degree in a related specialty and soon received a promotion.

Things clicked along happily for Luisa until she started a family. Then she found herself with two children, a busy home life, and a career that was demanding too much of her time. Luisa decided she needed a job that would give her more flexibility in her schedule.

She left the university to work part time for a home furnishings company, selling and installing window treatments.

For a while, Luisa felt this new work arrangement would be successful for her. It gave her flexibility in her schedule, and the number of hours she worked each week was more reasonable than her full-time job had been at the university. Yet after two years in her new position, something just didn't feel right to Luisa. She reviewed her CAP and realized that the type of work she was involved in—selling and supporting window treatments—didn't feel significant to her. In comparison, she'd loved the meaningfulness of her work with students at the university.

Determined to advance her career closer to her ideals, Luisa decided to seek out a position at the university—again, working with students—but this time finding a job that would allow her to work part time to better maintain her family balance at home. Within three months, she'd found and landed a position that met her criteria. She immediately felt as if her career was on track and advancing on the right path for her.

Core Courage Concept

Career advancement can feel like an ongoing series of course corrections, missteps, and successes. For the Career Coward, it can feel overwhelming and never-ending. Yet by focusing on a career advancement plan that is genuinely inspiring to you, and taking small steps to keep moving forward, you can attain impressive accomplishments over time. The result: career advancement that is meaningful and rewarding for you.

Confidence Checklist

☐ Review and revise your career advancement plan.

☐ Make steady progress on your CAP action items.

☐ Develop and maintain a success database.

☐ Take occasional trips outside your comfort zone.

Index